The Waterloo Papers
1815 and beyond

EDITED BY EDWARD OWEN

1997
AQ & DJ Publications

ISBN 0 904066 35 5

Designed and published by
AQ & DJ Publications
1 West Street, Tavistock, Devon PL19 8DS
Tel: (01822) 613577 Fax: (01822) 612785

Typeset by Elite Typesetting Techniques, Hampshire, England
Printed by Antony Rowe Ltd, Chippenham, Wiltshire, England

Contents

Illustrations

The portrait of the Duke of Wellington on the front cover was painted in 1804 by Robert Home (1752-1834) and is reproduced by courtesy of the National Portrait Gallery, London.

The portrait of Napoleon Bonaparte on the back cover is after Gérard and is reproduced by courtesy of the V & A Picture Library, London.

The map which provides the background for the cover is from *Waterloo: a guide to the Battlefield* and is reproduced by courtesy of Pitkin Pictorials.

We are grateful to the Rt Reverend Michael Mann, Dean of Windsor for his permission to reproduce an illustration and two diagrammatic maps from his book *And They Rode On.*

The illustration of 'Left Parry' on page 41 from Michael Mann's book *And They Rode On* is reproduced courtesy of the Royal Dragoon Guards Museum.

The illustration on page 24 of an Officer of the 1st King's Dragoon Guards is by J. Duplessi Bertaux 1816, published in Paris and is reproduced by courtesy of the Trustees for R G Hollins-Smith.

The line illustrations at the end of chapters were originally part of a toy theatre version of *The Battle of Waterloo* published by Redington and Pollock, lineal antecedents of Pollocks Toy Theatres. The original Battle of Waterloo entertainment on which these toy theatre versions were based, was first performed in Astley's Amphitheatre, on the south of the Thames, opposite the Houses of Parliament, in 1824.

Preface

A work such as this needs much outside help. First of all, I am most grateful to Mr McAvoy who discovered these papers, and to the National Army Museum for granting me the copyright.

Don Bridge, the Editor of Army Quarterly & Defence Journal, *together with his staff, have been more than helpful, not only with suggestions but also with compiling the footnotes and many other editorial tasks avoided by me!*

Dr Peter Boyden of the National Army Museum gave much useful advice. My gratitude also goes to others, especially to Lady Longford, Lord Anglesey and Lord Raglan. They are also mentioned in the Introduction

EDWARD OWEN

INTRODUCTION

by Edward Owen

This book is different from the usual run of Waterloo books. First, it is by no means all about the battle but describes incidents both before and after. Second, a great fascination lies in the circumstances in which the material was found.

In July 1965 a Mr John McAvoy, an Estate Agent and Factor in Inverness, wrote to the Director of the National Army Museum, then at Sandhurst, saying that he had in his possession a bound manuscript book containing letters and accounts of the battle and other events which he thought might be of interest to the Museum.

It was presumed that the book was discovered during a house clearance and in this way came into Mr McAvoy's possession. No connection with any person or house in Scotland was indicated and further information regarding its origin has proved impossible to obtain.

The contents of this book are written in a fine clerkly hand by the same person, probably about 1820. The writing is not easy to decipher and the cover of the manuscript book is plain and unremarkable. It therefore remained among the archives of the National Army Museum both at Sandhurst and at the present site in Royal Hospital Road until about ten years later. It was then discovered by the present writer who was at the time acting as volunteer archivist at the Museum. Being an avid student of the period he realised the importance of the find since some of the material, whilst certainly known, had probably never been published.

A further problem lay in the fact that letters were written under initials. There were divergencies in the spelling of proper names and in one case no trace of a writer could be found in any book of contemporary military records. These discrepancies and divergencies remain in the transcript published here although, where possible, footnotes attempt to find the 'correct' spelling or meaning.

Considerable research was involved and much encouragement and help was received from the Countess of Longford, the Marquess of Anglesey and Lord Raglan.

From the foregoing it may be seen that the Editor is not just another Waterloo historian but merely the interpreter of much new and fascinating material which has been discovered by the merest chance.

It has already been stated that there was a considerable problem of identities, those of Allan, "B.S." and "T.S." being the most important.

In Chapter II, Allan is spelt Allen; this is certainly a fault of transcription.

In July 1815 James Allan of the 94th Regiment, then known as the "Scotch Brigade" became Military Secretary to the Duke of Wellington in place of Lord Fitzroy Somerset who had lost an arm at Waterloo.

Allan himself was not at Waterloo but had served with Wellington in India and in the Peninsula. He is known to have kept a diary and it would appear that most of the letters and papers found in the Manuscript book were either collected or requested by him to enlarge his records.

Where this diary is today is not known for certain. No record that it has ever been published can be found. The value of the information contained in the Manuscript book is therefore greatly enhanced.

In the select Bibliography under Published Sources in Elizabeth Longford's *Wellington – The Years of the Sword*, the following note appears: Allan, General. Extracts from diary published by Lt Col J.G.O. Whitehead, *Army Quarterly* October 1965. There is no note in the *Army Quarterly* of that date and lady Longford has no recollection of the diary or where it might be now!

B.S. and T.S. are two brothers, Benjamin and Thomas Sydenham. They were sons of Major General Sydenham of the Madras Establishment. Benjamin, the elder son, had joned the "family" of the Marquess Wellesley, Wellington's elder brother and Governor General of India, in 1801. Shortly afterwards, he was sent to England with special despatches and a note to Lord Bathurst saying "His peculiarly good conduct under my brother Colonel Wellesley during the war (against Tipu Sultan) originally recommended him to my notice... His talents and temper are uncommonly excellent and he possesses very extensive information on every subject connected with our military and political interest in India".

Thomas, the younger and better known son became much involved in the remarkably complicated life of Lord Wellesley and also served for a time on Wellington's staff in the Peninsula. They were therefore both closely connected with both "the elder brother" and the Duke hence the use of Arthur and Padrone[(1)] in references to Wellington.

The younger died first in 1816 aged 37 and the elder in 1828 aged 52. Both suffered severely in health. Obituary notices of the two brothers appear as appendices.

Short character sketches of Wellington and Napoleon by the Editor are also included as appendices, as is one of Lord Whitworth the British Ambassador to France during the Peace of Amiens 1802-3. This latter account has been largely taken from the *Dictionary of National Biography*. Information regarding others mentioned in the text appears either in chapter headings or in note form. The texts have not been altered except in the interests of clarity, punctuation and certain archaic spellings. Capitals were used in Germanic profusion and Bonaparte has been substituted for Buonaparte which was used throughout.

The chapters are, as far as is possible, in chronological order but not necessarily in the order in which they appear in the Manuscript Book, the contents of which form the subject matter of this work. Two are undated. Chapter VI covers a period from 5 July – 11 August as the contents form a complete letter.

Each chapter has a descriptive heading and introduction if the subject matter makes this necessary.

---

(1) "Padrone" – a nickname sometimes attached to Wellington, meaning a patron or benefactor or probably in this case a father figure.

British Infantry

CHAPTER ONE

An interview between Napoleon as First Consul and Lord Whitworth, the British Ambassador 13 March 1803 The scene: a reception in the Tuileries gardens

The first episode in this book is a story that has often been told. It reads here like an eye-witness account and is reminiscent of the scene many years later between Napoleon and Talleyrand, which led Talleyrand to say what a pity it was that so great a man had been so badly brought up.

On 13th March, 1803, during the Peace of Amiens which had been made just a year earlier Napoleon, the First Consul, accuses England of wishing to renew the war. England is represented by Lord Whitworth,(1) *the Ambassador.*

Neither side had kept the terms of the Peace but up to this moment these lapses had been played down by both sides. Napoleon now in front of the whole Diplomatic Corps, bursts into one of his famous rages and creates a scene which Whitworth handles with considerable tact. This scene, obviously contrived, marks a crisis both in the career of Napoleon and also in the history of England, since it makes a further outbreak of war inevitable.

The description of what takes place is written in French which has been translated.

Yesterday, in the great circle before all the Ambassadors and Foreign Ministers, Bonaparte, flushed with rage and agitation, went up to Lord Whitworth and said:- "Have you any news from England?"

Lord Whitworth answered "Yes, I have had letters from the Secretary of State informing me of his Majesty's communication to you".

"Do you want war?" said Bonapart.

"No, God preserve us from so great a calamity" the Ambassador replied.

Bonapart continued by saying "It would be thought that one war lasting fifteen years would be enough, but if you want another fifteen years I will oblige you. You are now arming and so I too must arm".

Lord Whitworth then said that the First Consul knew very well that even precautionary measures could not be taken secretly in England and that the consent of Parliament was needed to put the country in a state of defence; that England certainly did not want war and would do everything in her power to avoid such a calamity.

All this was delivered on the part of our Ambassador with mildness and at the same time calm dignity highly becoming his situation, to which his noble figure added very considerably...

Bonapart went from him in a flutter and in going round the circle kept muttering half aloud as if he was beside himself. He came back to Lord Whitworth and said "What good will arming do you and under what pretext are you so doing? You know that I have no ships of the line in commission and therefore woe to the first of our two nations to break the Treaty of Amiens".(2)

He broke away pulling the door after him as if in a passion – his Aides de Camp who remained and the whole circle witnessed all.

The Ambassadors present surrounded Lord Whitworth and without much restraint expressed their astonishment and disapprobation of the man, by laughing and shrugging their shoulders. Today, Paris rings with high praise of Lord Whitworth's conduct and speaks with ill-humour and disgust of the other.

---

(1) Lord Whitworth. See Appendix 3.

(2) Treaty of Amiens. Two poor harvests, the fall of Pitt's administration and French successes at Copenhagen and in Egypt led the British Government to seek a general peace with France in 1801. Negotiations were led for France by Joseph Bonaparte and he conceded very little. Napoleon himself regarded the peace treaty merely as a breathing space and it lasted barely a year.

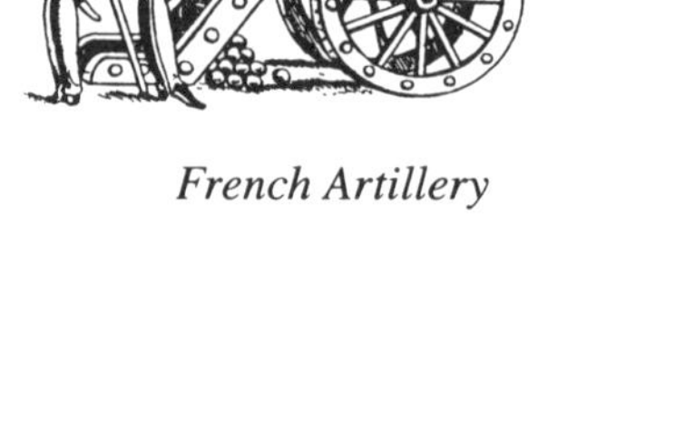

French Artillery

CHAPTER TWO

Letter from Ben Sydenham to Allen (sic) regarding the Convention of Cintra and Wellesley's part therein 27 September 1808

There is no further material until 1808, when a letter appears regarding Sir Arthur Wellesley's part in the Convention of Cintra.[1]

On 21st August, 1808, Wellesley's defeat of Junot at Vimiero[2] *had been marred by the failure of Sir Harry Burrard to follow up the victory. Sir Harry, who had landed in Portugal only at 9 a.m. on the morning of the battle, was the senior officer but had waived his right to command until the battle was over. He then resolutely refused to push forward. It can only be said for that unfortunate man that he acted according to the best of his judgement and that he was in a most unfair position. Had he acted on Wellesley's advice and had all gone well Wellesley would have received the credits, but if anything had gone wrong, he himself would have been held to blame.*

His term of command was short, so that he had no opportunity to atone for his mistake. Early on the following morning Sir Hew Dalrymple, the Governor of Gibraltar, landed and took command. Sir Hew was not at his ease. He had never served as a general officer in the field, and had not seen active operations since 1794. Wellesley at once laid his plans before Dalrymple and pressed him to advance. Dalrymple was not however disposed after a few hours' command of a strange army in a strange country to risk an operation. The interview was not pleasant. Wellesley considered Dalrymple to be "prejudiced against any opinions that he might give him".

London 27 Sept. 1808

My dear Allen, (sic)

I have not written to you for some time, not only because I have been continually on the wing, backwards and forwards from Ramsgate, but because it was impossible for me to send you anything certain about Arthur Wellesley and the

Convention which still occupies everybody's attention. It has excited universal indignation, such a ferment has never existed. It is worse than ever on receipt of Whitelock's disaster. All that I know is this and you may depend on my accuracy as I have read all Arthur's private letters.

The Generals-in-Chief uniformly overruled all Arthur's plans. Firstly, Burrard would not allow him to march on the 20th instead of waiting to be attacked. Secondly, Burrard would not allow corps to be landed at Figueras and to be marched to Santarem in order to cut off Junot's retreat. On the contrary when Moore began to disembark his men in consequence of letters from Arthur Wellesley he ordered them to re-embark and to come round to Maccira where they could not obtain supplies. Thirdly, Burrard would not allow Arthur to follow up the victory of the 21st by an immediate pursuit of the enemy.

I have seen a letter from Moore in which he says "If this had been done in the way proposed by Sir Arthur Wellesley the whole French army must have been annihilated".

Fourthly, Sir Arthur was not at all consulted about the Armistice. It was negotiated by Dalrymple or rather dictated by Kellerman. Arthur *neither wrote, approved* or negotiated it. Sir Hew intended to have signed it himself but Kellerman requested that Sir Arthur might sign it and he did so by Dalrymple's desire. Afterwards Dalrymple wished to send him to Sir C. Cotton but the French would not let him go because he objected so strongly to (the) armistice.

However notwithstanding all this he will never, I fear, get over *his signature.*[3] The King is outrageous (sic) about it and neither he (Wellesley) or his army will receive any honours. Had this not happened he would, I hear, have been a Viscount with a pension and the command of the army in Spain. He is now not recalled *and that is all.*

Dalrymple is recalled and is considered to be the responsible person. It is a sad business and has given us all the greatest affliction. Pole is completely depressed. Lord Wellesley is gone back to Ramsgate and holds up against it very well. [He thinks the case very clear as far as Arthur is concerned.] Henry came to town for a day but is returned to Suffolk. I am going back to Ramsgate. I have not a word of news. I hope Mrs. A(llan) is well and that you continue to be pleased with your excursion.

Yours ever etc. etc.

B.S.

Arthur is adored by the army. All the generals including Moore have written home about him in the highest terms.

---

(1) The Convention of Cintra, 22 August 1808. After Wellington's victory over Junot at Vimiero in Portugal, terms were negotiated by the more senior generals, Burrard and Dalrymple. So ably led was the French negotiating team that they secured terms which included free evacuation and repatriation for 26,000 troops and baggage using British shipping. These easy terms caused outrage in England and all three British commanders were recalled to London to face a court of enquiry.

(2) The Battle of Vimiero 21 August 1808. Wellesley's men drove back the French Commander in Chief in Portugal, General Junot. Wellesley was forbidden by his senior commander, General Burrard, to pursue the French troops. Later Burrard and General Dalrymple negotiated the Convention of Cintra, the terms of which were so favourable to the French that all three generals were recalled to London for an enquiry.

(3) Wellington was obliged to sign the treaty although by instinct he was against doing so.

Field Piece

CHAPTER THREE

Lord Fitzroy Somerset's Account of the events from 15 – 18 June 1815

The account which follows is Lord Fitzroy Somerset's description of the events from 15-18 June, and is probably the most important narrative among these papers.

It must be remembered that Somerset was Wellington's Military Secretary. Until he had his arm shot off later in the battle, he was naturally close to his commander's side and would be well acquainted with his orders.

As Lord Raglan he commanded the British Army in the Crimea until his death on service in 1855. Much has been written about this charming but unfortunate man. He was probably more sinned against than sinning and inherited years of Horse Guards' muddle. Except for an unfortunate habit of referring to the Russians as the French, who in the Crimean War happened to be our allies, he did his best under intolerable conditions.

The most interesting disclosure in the narrative is Somerset's description of how DeLancey (the Quartermaster General) who subsequently died of wounds, was sent from Quatre Bras to reconnoitre a new position to cover Brussels. This is certainly contrary to the old belief that the Duke, some short time before, had noted the Mont St Jean position and had also, with his thumbnail, marked on a map this position while talking to the Duke of Richmond at the famous ball.

15th June, 1815 About five o'clock in the afternoon the Duke of Wellington while at dinner received from the Prince of Orange(1), who was at Braine le Compte, a report sent to His Royal Highness from his advanced posts, (probably from Mons or L'Eveque), informing him that the French had attacked the Prussians' advanced posts on the Sambre. The Duke immediately directed the Quarter Master General, (Colonel DeLancey), to send orders for the troops to assemble at the headquarters of their respective divisions and to be in readiness to march at the shortest notice.

5th Division consisted of the

8th British Brigade	Kempt
9th British Brigade	Pack
5th Household Brigade	

This division under Picton[(2)], who had arrived only that morning, was at Brussels.

The Brunswick troops under the Duke of Brunswick were at Laeken about two miles from Brussels and the contingent of Nassau[(3)] was in the neighbourhood.

These troops were ordered to hold themselves in readiness to march at a moments notice.

Lord Fitzroy Somerset, who was at his own quarters, being informed of this intelligence went directly to headquarters. He found the Duke in the Park giving the necessary orders to those around him. He wished everything to be in readiness to move in a moment but was waiting for further information of the motions of the enemy before he made a decided movement with my (sic) part of his army, it being of the utmost consequence first to ascertain the point to which Bonaparte directed his operations.

About ten o'clock at night Lord Fitzroy Somerset talking with the Duke about the French observed "No doubt we shall be able to manage these fellows". The Duke said "There was little doubt of that provided he did not make a false movement" and he told the QMG that the troops must not be ordered to march till further information was received.

The Duchess of Richmond had a ball that night and as it was the place where every British officer of rank was likely to be found, perhaps for that reason the Duke dressed and went there.

The Prince of Orange having remained at his post until a certain hour in the evening, hearing nothing from his advanced posts and everything being quiet in his front and probably considering the attack on the Prussian outposts of not much importance, went also to the Duchess of Richmond's. The Duke told him there that he thought he might be required at his post and advised him to return, which the Prince did.

The Earl of Uxbridge and a great many cavalry officers were at the ball too, but before midnight went away to their respective quarters.

Further reports reached the Duke in the course of the evening from the Prussians, sent by Sir Henry Harding to General Muffling[(4)], which determined the Duke to send orders to the British on the right to march to their left (on Nivelles and Quartre Bras). Lord Hill's Aide-de-camp carried the orders to his Lordship.

Picton's division paraded in the Park and about four o'clock in the morning 16th June marched out of Brussels followed by the Brunswickers[(5)] and the contingent of Nassau and moved along the highroad to Charleroi through the forest of Soignies. These troops halted a short time between the forest and the village of Waterloo.

16th June The Duke left Brussels about eight o'clock in the morning and proceded as quickly as possible to Quatre Bras where he arrived at about ten o'clock.

As he passed Picton, he ordered the 5th Division, Brunswick and Nassau troops to resume their march which they did, between twelve and one o'clock.

As the Duke was on his way to Quatre Bras he was informed that Prince Weimar, with the Brigade of Nassau Troops, had been driven from Frasne on the preceding evening and had been forced to fall back beyond Quatre Bras and had lost the communication between our left and Blücher's[(6)] position by the road from Nivelles and Quatre Bras to Namur. But the French afterwards retired.

Early in the morning the Prince of Orange reinforced Prince Weimar with Perponcher's Division of Infantry and regained, or rather re-occupied the ground which the Nassau Brigade had lost the evening before.

When the Duke arrived at Quatre Bras he found the Prince of Orange there. He observed only a few of the enemy in front who occassionally fired a shot and a little popping musketry but nothing more serious was at that time threatened in that quarter.

The Duke accompanied by his staff and a small escort of cavalry rode from Quatre Bras between eleven and twelve o'clock to Blücher's position. The Marshal was at Batti St. Croix. The Prussian troops were formed in close column on the heights in rear of St. Amand and Ligny, which were occupied, and the left of the Prussian army extended beyond Sombreff.

The Duke and Blücher saw the French in great force advancing towards the Prussians and the Duke observed to Blücher he would soon be attacked.

16th June. The Duke expecting that our cavalry, the remainder of the Prince of Orange's corps, the Guards and Allen's division would arrive at Quatre Bras about

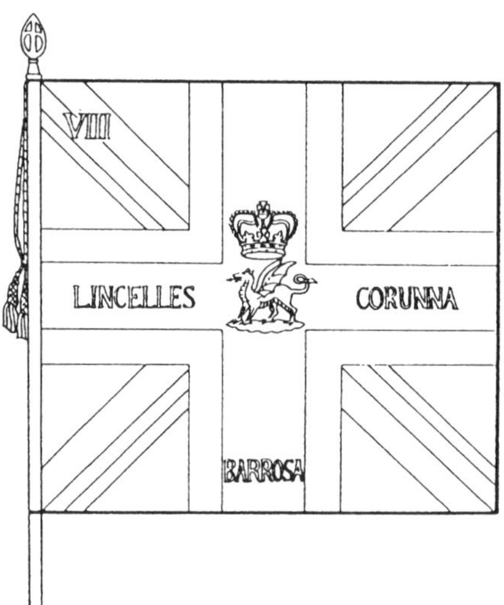

Britain: Regimental (8th Company's) Colour, 3rd Bn., 1st Foot Guards, as carried at Waterloo. 1814 issue.

Britain: King's (Colonel's) Colour, 2nd Foot Guards, carried by the 2nd Bn. at Waterloo. 1814 issue.

two o'clock, told Blücher that he would give him all the support in his power and the Duke galloped back Quatre Bras which he reached about half-past two. He looked attentively with his spy-glass and observing the movements of the French towards Frasne told the Prince of Orange he would be attacked directly.

In a few minutes the French advanced and charged the Prince of Orange. Picton by this time had come up and passing Quatre Bras had formed about six or seven hundred yards in front of it, on the left of the high road leading to Frasne and Charleroi.

The 42nd on the right (Pack) was charged by the French cavalry. The Duke brought forward the Belgic light cavalry just arrived.

The Duke asked the Prince of Orange what troops were in the wood on the right of the road and of Picton's right flank. The Prince said – those of Nassau. Lord Fitzroy Somerset asked the same question of Abercromby, the Prince's QMG, who made the same answer.

The wood had been occupied by Belgian troops but they had been driven out of it by the French and had retired to right and rear. To the surprise of everybody French troops were seen coming out of the wood and were at first taken for Belgians.

The French cavalry charged the Belgian cavalry and dispersed them — they went to the rear. The carts, etc. coming up along the highroad from Brussels took the alarm, turned round and went back with followers etc. in the greatest confusion.

Many of the Belgic cavalry went to Brussels and spread the alarm. The Duke and Lord Fitzroy Somerset were in front when the French cavalry charged the Belgic cavalry and with difficulty got back to the 92nd, posted at Quatre Bras. The Duke leaped a bank and ditch, and on a worse horse he might not have escaped.

The French cavalry suffered much from the fire of the 92nd, not only as they passed the right flank of the regiment, but also in coming out of a farm yard into which they had got in the rear and in getting back to their own positions.

The Prince of Orange exerted himself greatly. He was at one time surrounded by the enemy but was rescued by the gallantry of the Belgians. It was on this occasion he took off the insignia of his order and threw it among the men saying "You have all deserved it". They fastened it to their colours and with one voice cried, "Long live our Prince", and swore to defend it till death.

The Duke of Brunswick was killed when Picton's division first moved forward in front of Quatre Bras. The troops advanced with too much rapidity and lost their order. The Duke of Wellington sent Lord Fitzroy Somerset to the commanding officers to order them to keep their troops in hand. Kempt observed to Lord Fitzroy Somerset that they were certainly not in hand but that he would get them in hand as soon as possible, which was soon done.

The Guards arrived about five o'clock in the afternoon from Nivelles. It had been the Duke's intention to have attacked the enemy as soon as the guards arrived, but finding the wood in possession of the enemy he gave up the idea as the right flank of our troops would have been quite exposed.

The Guards were ordered to drive the enemy from the woods and in doing so they lost about five hundred men — not perhaps going about it as a Rifle or Light

Corps would have done.

The French were driven from the wood and finally repulsed at all points.

They retired about dusk to a rising ground two miles distant, with a wood in their rear. A hollow ground separated them from Picton, who held the rising ground in front of and to the left of the road from Quatre Bras.

The firing on the left towards the Prussians had ceased and the Duke about nine o'clock at night left Quatre Bras for Genappe, where supper had been ordered at the inn. Riding along and conceiving Blücher had repulsed the French, the Duke observed "He was a damned fine old fellow".

Captain Harding came to Genappe about half past ten in the evening from Blücher's army for a surgeon to dress his brother, Sir Henry Harding, whose hand had been shot off.

The Duke enquired when he had left the ground: [he] said between eight and nine o'clock when he thought the Prussians had suffered severely, that there was considerable confusion [and] that he saw many Prussian soldiers in small parties of two and three crossing the corn fields to the rear, but that he could not say the Prussians were defeated for they still held their positions.

The Duke did not altogether rely on this information, at least not to its full extent, thinking that a young officer agitated perhaps on account of his brother might have considered things worse than they were.

Indeed, so little was it conceived that the French had gained any advantage that Lord Fitzroy Somerset, at half past ten wrote to Lady Fitzroy Somerset in Brussels "that the Prussians had repulsed the French". The Duke went to sleep at Genappe between eleven and twelve o'clock. The staff were employed by the Duke's orders, writing or despatching letters to a late hour. About two o'clock in the morning a courier arrived from Brussels, but with no particular intelligence.

17th June. The Duke got on horseback about three o'clock in the morning and proceeded to Quatre Bras. He immediately despatched Sir A Gordon with a troop of cavalry to patrol towards the Prussian army to ascertain what had really happened. About seven o'clock Sir A Gordon returned to Quatre Bras having only seen a few of the enemy's vedettes who retired as he advanced. But he brought information that Blücher had been obliged to retire upon Wavre. Everybody at Headquarters conceived that it was a place a little in the rear of the Prussian position, no one at this instant recollecting the precise situation of Wavre, in reality so far distant in the rear. It did not occur to any person that the Prussians could have fallen back so far. General Muffling was the person who opened the Duke's eyes. Upon being told the Prussians had fallen back on Wavre [he] observed "Ma foi c'est bien loin"(7), and the Duke immediately resolved on making a corresponding movement and to fall back on the road to Brussels.

He sent off the worse troops first; Belgians, Nassaus and Dutch. The Brunswickers, Hanoverians and British followed. He gave orders to Lord Hill, who had arrived at Quatre Bras in advance of his troops, to make his Corps retrograde from Nivelles by the high road leading to Brussels. He despatched DeLancey, the

QMG, to mark out a position in front of the Forest of Soignies, which the Duke proposed to take up with his army.

The troops began to move from Quatre Bras about nine o'clock. Part of Alten's brigade marched on the right of the high road which it was desirable to leave as free and as little encumbered as possible.

About two o'clock in the afternoon the French cavalry showed themselves in force on the high road leading from Namur, turning off from it to the right about half-a-mile from Quatre Bras.

In a few moments afterwards they showed some artillery and fired some shells. All our infantry had fallen back. A Light Corps which with the cavalry had remained, covered the line of march. The Duke told Lord Uxbridge that it was of no purpose to wait: the sooner he got away the better: that no time was to be lost in getting off.

The Duke left Quatre Bras between two and three o'clock and proceeded leisurely towards Waterloo. On arriving near La Belle Alliance he thought it was the position the QMG would have taken up, being the most commanding ground, but [the QMG] had found it too extended to be occupied by our troops so had proceeded further on and marked out a position. This was to the right near Braine l'Allend(8) thence to the left across the high road which joined on the rear near Mont St Jean.

About four o'clock the Duke found the troops on that spot. On looking at the position, finding the ground between Braine l'Allend and Hougoumont broken, he ordered the right to be thrown back [to] the angle or elbow in the rear of Hougoumont and the extreme right on Marbe Braine, intending that Braine l'Allend should be occupied by a battery.

The infantry had been conducted to their respective stations by the staff officers. The cavalry covering the whole were closely followed by the French cavalry and guns.

Our artillery fired from our position on the enemy: this was about seven o'clock in the evening. The Duke was very angry, not wishing to provoke hostilities, and ordered the firing to cease. The French fired from a few guns and about eight o'clock drew off.

Our troops bivouacked a little in the rear of the position marked out for the line and the Duke proceeded to Waterloo, where he slept.

18th June. The Duke rose between two and three o'clock in the morning, [and] wrote to the Duc de Beri at Alost not to move from that place on the idle reports of the movements of the enemy, but if he had any official information that we had evacuated Brussels and that it was occupied by the French, in that case to proceed to the Tête de Flandres (on the Scheldt towards Antwerp). The Duke de Beri did not wait for official information: he set off at once for Antwerp. The Duke wrote also to the Governor of Antwerp to admit women and others into the town.

About six o'clock the Duke got on horseback on his way to the front of the line. He met a Prussian officer who came from Blücher, in consequence of the Duke having the night before sent to him for one or two Prussian corps to support him.

Blücher promised to do so.

The Duke proceeded to the right and looked at the ground on which Clinton's Division was posted, then went to Hougoumont, gave some directions about into which (state) it was to be put [sic]: ordered Colonel Cooke[9] to make loop holes in the wall: to throw down part of the garden wall: to raise a temporary rampart within it that the troops might be able to fire over it and to throw an abbatis[10] across the Nivelles Road beyond Hougoumont.

The Duke rode unaccompanied up to the high ground on the Nivelles Road to reconnoitre the ground: there were at that time two or three companies of Mitchell's brigade on the high ground and vedettes beyond them.

The 3rd Division was at first brought in front of the cross roads and then brought back to the rear of it. Two brigades of artillery (12 pieces) to each division and in front of it a brigade of howitzers at the elbow in front of the Guards.

The French reconnoitred the right of our position, the Duke went to the left to La Haye and a road to Dendemonde.

The Duke was in front of the left of the Guards when the action began. He gave orders frequently to the Prince of Orange in person for the movement and formation of the corps, but when things went on he gave orders to commanders of divisions and corps.

In the attack on Hougoumont all our guns opened on the French column. They were stopped by the fire of our artillery: for a quarter of an hour nothing was done.

The Duke observed "We have stopped them". As the French advanced towards Hougoumont, the Nassau troops, eight hundred, quitted the orchard which was then occupied by Lord Saltoun. The French made a second attempt and were again stopped.

In a third attempt they got into the wood. These attacks were all made under cover of artillery, but without cavalry: the attacks lasted more than an hour and a half: the Duke watched these attacks.

The Coldstream moved down in line to the right of Hougoumont by the high road, because the French were getting on the left of it.

After these attacks on Hougoumont the Duke went to the centre near the Tree[11] on the right of the high road to Belle Alliance before two o'clock and saw the attack on Picton's division.

On the advance of the French, the 95th, which was posted at the quarry on the left of the road and above La Haye Sainte, was withdrawn.

The French attacked in three columns, Pack, Kempt and the Hanoverians. They ascended, formed in line and moved up to the hedge behind which Picton's division was posted and were repulsed.

Ponsonby's brigade charged the French columns. He was killed far in front of our line. The 12th Regiment, Vandeleur's brigade charged also: Colonel Ponsonby, commanding it, was killed. At this time our artillery were in rear of the hedge. The cuirassiers charged Halkett's brigade, the 30th and 73rd, upon which Lord Edward Somerset with the Household Brigade charged the enemy. He went himself to the right of the farm of La Haye Sainte; many of the cuirassiers were killed near the wall of the farm; another regiment charged to the left of the farm and to the left of the high road (the brigade crossed the high road inclining to the right).

The brigade, or part of it, advanced a great deal too far, got into the position of the enemy near La Belle Alliance and suffered much.

The French gained possession of La Haye Sainte and fired upon our troops from the upper part of the house.

An officer of cuirassiers came over to us, and was brought up to the Duke by Churchill, Lord Hill's ADC. He reported that Bonaparte was going to make a great effort with his cavalry. This was about three or four o'clock.

There were frequent charges by cuirassiers, dragoons and lancers. They were repeatedly driven back by our cavalry. They continued for two or three hours. The great effort of the enemy's cavalry was between three and four o'clock: no infantry. Our limbers(12) were drawn to the rear, the guns left in front. The Duke thought Bonaparte guilty of a great fault in not attacking with infantry also at the same time.

The charges were between La Haye Sainte and Hougoumont. The Brunswickers were by degrees brought up, some on the right, some on the left of the Guards. As the French infantry advanced, they saw nothing but our guns, (the infantry were behind the crest of the ridge). The Duke said, "I'll be damned if we shall not lose this ground if we do not take care". This ground was between Halkett's brigade and the Guards: the troops were much thinned.

The Duke ordered the Guards to take ground to their left towards Halkett's brigade. He sent orders for Adam's brigade and Mitchell's to be brought across the Nivelles road. The Duke went to Adam and made him form his brigade in line four deep. With this brigade the Duke crowned the crest of the hill before the French infantry came up to it. Adam moved on the right of the Guards and advanced beyond the line of our infantry, at that time all exposed and suffering much from musketry as well as from the enemy's artillery.

The Guards crossed the road and formed in front of it. Three weak battalions of Halkett's brigade did not reach the high road on their left. Adam had got rather too forward with his brigade, which he was aware of before the Duke's order to fall back.

Lord Fitzroy Somerset told the Duke that our troops did not fill the ground on the left of the Guards to the high road. The Duke went to the Guards and made them take ground to their left.

Lord Fitzroy Somerset was wounded about seven o'clock, a musket ball from La Haye Sainte. Half an hour after he quitted the field.

Another heavy attack was made by the French Guards upon our Guards and Adam's brigade, by whom they were repulsed. After this the Duke looked attentively through his glass and observed great confusion in the French army. He said he would advance.

In addition to this Lord Fitzroy Somerset wrote the following note:-

Badminton, 17 January 1816

My dear Sir,

I enclose a copy of the return which I made out some little time before the Battle of Waterloo and which I told you I would get from Paris.

I hope it will be useful to you and you are welcome to it.

Yours, etc

F.S.

I add a short memorandum of our probable force on the 18th. In the calculation of our loss on the 16th and 17th, I have allowed a little for panic.

Grand total of the present return		75,975
Not in action Colville's division	2 brigades	
with the Prince of Orange	4,330	
Dutch infantry with ditto	10,400	
Estoff's brigade of cavalry	937	
At Braine l'Allend Dutch division		
belonging to the left Corps	6,000	
Probable loss and casualties between 16th and 18th June		25,667(13)
Probable force on the 18th June		50,308

---

(1) The Prince of Orange (1792-1844). Eldest son of William I of Holland, he later became William II of Holland. He commanded a corps in Wellington's army and was wounded at Waterloo.

(2) Lt Gen Sir Thomas Picton (1758-1815) commanded the veteran 5th Division during the Campaign of the Hundred Days, fighting at Quatre Bras. He was killed on 18 June 1815 leading his men to the charge at Waterloo.

(3) Contingent of Nassau. Part of the Netherlands Army. In this transcript, the Nassauers (correct spelling) are referred to as Nassaus.

(4) Major (later General) Carl von Muffling, Baron. As a colonel, he served as Blücher's Deputy Chief of Staff during the Waterloo campaign and was Prussian liaison officer

attached to Wellington's staff during the critical days. He was author of the book *History of the Campaign of 1815* first published in 1816 and republished by Wakefield in 1970.

(5) "Brunswickers" – men from Brunswick. A corps of 700 volunteer Hussars, commanded by Frederick William Duke of Brunswick who died at Quatre Bras in 1815.

(6) Field Marshal Gebhard von Blücher (1742-1819) was Commander of the Prussian troops at Waterloo. Known to his men as 'Old Forward' or 'Marshal Forward' for his personal bravery, he was an active patriot and in the War of German Liberation he defeated the French as Commander in Chief at Leipzig (1813). His army's arrival at Waterloo on the afternoon of June 18, threatening the French flank and rear absorbed Napoleon's reserves at a critical moment and played a crucial part in Wellington's victory.

(7) "Ma foi c'est bien loin" – My God, that is a long way away".

(8) Braine Le Leude is spelt variously Braine L'Allend, Braine l'alleud, Braine Aleaud.

(9) Lieutenant General Sir George Cooke (1768-1837) commanded the Guard's Division at Waterloo and was awarded the KCB later in 1815. He was promoted Lt Gen in 1821.

(10) Abattis or Abatis – a fortification of felled trees with their branches pointing outwards. From the French word 'abattre' – to fell.

(11) "The Tree" – Duke of Wellington's tree, so called because he spent so much time standing beside or near it. It is mentioned in a number of books.

(12) Limber – part of a gun carriage (axle, pole and two wheels) which is attached to the back of a piece of equipment, e.g. field artillery.

(13) The difference in figures may arise through the inclusion of units not previously mentioned.

Sunday 18 June 1815
Timetable of the Battle

The battlefield, now on the outskirts of Brussels, is protected by law and still looks much the same as it did on Sunday 18 June 1815

THE ARMIES

Wellington
50,000 infantry
12,500 cavalry
5,500 gunners

A total of 68,000 allied troops – one-third British
156 guns

Blücher
89,000 Prussians
92 guns

Napoleon
49,000 infantry
15,750 cavalry
7,250 gunners

Total 72,000 French
246 guns

2 am Wellington received a message from Blücher saying he would reinforce him by late afternoon. Wellington only fought the battle on this understanding.

Phase 1
11.30 am Napoleon delayed starting to allow the ground to dry out after the night's heavy rain. French guns began to fire. Most of Wellington's troops were lying down behind the crest of Mont St. Jean and were protected. The Belgian-Dutch brigade in the open were decimated.

Phase 2
11.30 am The French advanced against Hougoumont, held by Guards Light companies. The French plan was to lure Wellington's reserve over to deal with this but he sent only a few reinforcements.

1 pm By now 2.5 French divisions were involved at Hougoumont. The British held firm even when the buildings were set on fire. This was the first French disaster.

Phase 3
From
1.30 or
2 pm Napoleon learned that the Prussians were coming, so sent VI Corps from his central reserve to create a defensive flank to the east at Fichermont/Plancenoit. Marshal Ney, in overall control of the actual fighting, ordered a French attack by one of Napoleon's main corps, under d'Erlon. Muddled orders put three of his four divisions into an unwise formation which attracted massive allied artillery fire. A French attempt to attack Picton's division on the French attempt to attack Picton's division on the ridge failed although Picton himself was killed.

Uxbridge then made a cavalry charge and routed the French. The Scots Greys captured a French tricolour, as did the Household Brigade.

The Scots Greys then overstretched themselves by attacking the French

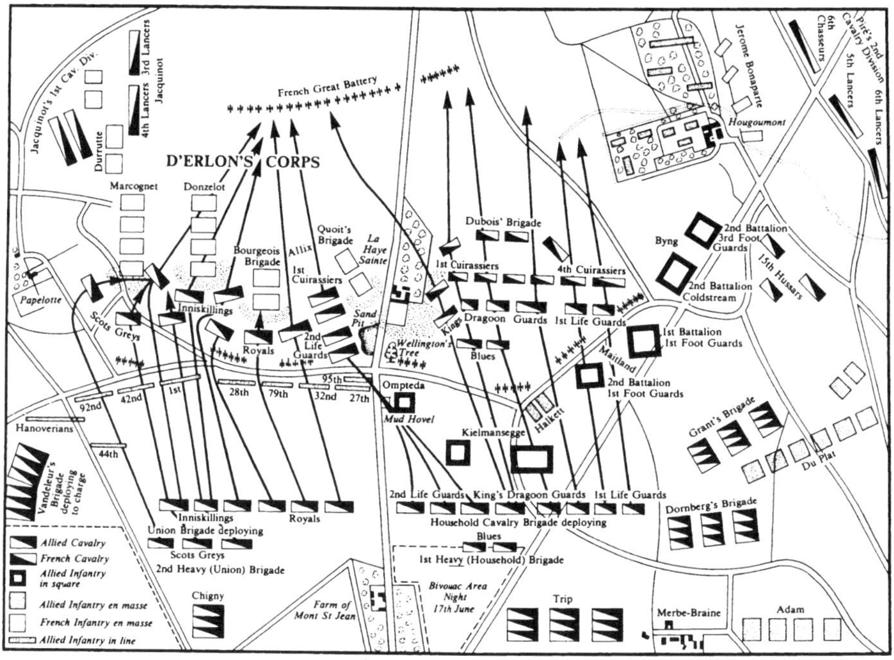

Situation at 2.30 p.m.

grand battery and were routed by French lancers as they were tried to get back to the Allied lines. The result was that, even though the French grand attack had failed, Wellington lost a third of his cavalry.

3 pm Meanwhile the garrison at La Haie Sainte – 376 Hanoverians of the King's German Legion under Major George Baring, were beating off heavy French attacks and standing firm.

Phase 4
From 3.30
or 4 pm
onwards Prussians began to arrive opposite Plancenoit. The French launched a cavalry charge against Wellington's right centre, believing he was evacuating his position. Most of the cavalry became involved, but with no infantry or artillery backup. Wellington's troops formed squares and held firm. The French were soundly beaten and retreated.

5.30 pm There was a lull in the fighting. The Prussians had now been joined by Blücher himself with more troops. Fighting followed and the French eventually took Plancenoit using the Old Guard and most of the Young Guard. By now all French reserves were committed.

3 p.m. to nightfall

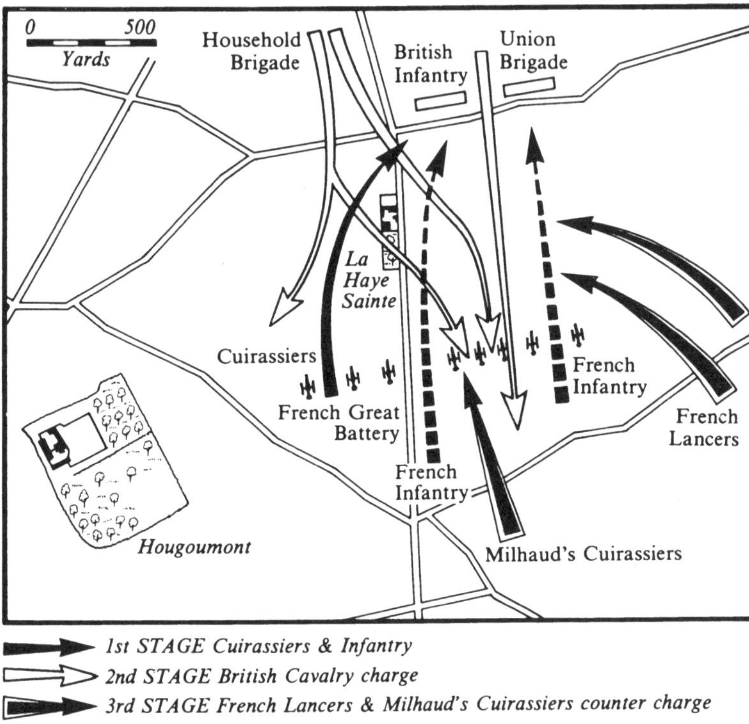

Phase 5

6 pm A second attack by the French on La Haie Sainte was successful as the defenders ran out of ammunition. Many were killed as they fled; only 41 survived. A co-ordinated attack by the French with artillery support caused Wellington's centre to waver. Wellington sent Vandeleur's cavalry to reinforce. Ney wanted to send in the Imperial Guard at this point, but it was over near Plancenoit.

7 pm An hour had passed in re-grouping. Wellington learned the remaining Prussians were approaching his left wing, so allied infantry units could be diverted to support the centre.

Phase 6

7 pm The Imperial Guard were now sent into action, first led by Napoleon, then by Ney. For some reason the columns veered to the west of La Haie Sainte and opposed Wellington's right centre. Here Guardsmen under Maitland were hidden in a cornfield. They stood up and fired, taking the French by surprise. The Prussians arrived and joined in.

Wellington charged with his whole line. The French retreat became a rout.

Napoleon fled towards Genappe and eventual captivity on St Helena.

9 pm Wellington and Blücher met at La Belle Alliance. Pursuit of the French lasted most of the night.

Total losses: Allies 22,000. French 41,000.

The main memorial to Belgian and Dutch troops is a large artificial hill with a lion on top. It is sited almost in the centre of what was Wellington's line.

French Soldiers

CHAPTER FOUR

An anonymous but very vivid account of the Waterloo Campaign Undated

This account of the Waterloo Campaign is anonymous. It is none the less interesting due to the vividness of the descriptions of the battle and also to the writer's obvious enthusiasm for "our side".

It was probably written by a combatant since as an account of the battle it has the limitations of someone who was unable to get an overall view of "both sides of the hill".

The Duke of Wellington is hardly mentioned, which however limited an account of the Battle of Waterloo may be, is most unusual.

The states of Europe represented in Congress were yet employed in re-establishing the basis of public order when Bonaparte suddenly appeared upon the shores of France. In a few days, after a march of unexampled triumph, he was once more seated on his Imperial throne and the Bourbons were again fugitives.

This revolution resembled less the course of political events than the illusory transitions of the stage.

Europe only a moment before was agitated merely by the conflicts of diplomatists. It became at once by common impulse the theatre of warlike preparation: the several parts of the great coalition flew together with magnetic force and all the nations armed and assembled their armies round the territories of France. Of these the Anglo-Prussian armies occupied the line between the fortresses of Tournai and Namur.

Bonaparte by a well concealed scheme resolved to strike a blow before the Allies had completed all their preparations and by judicious movements had on the 14th June concentrated between the Sambre and Meuse five corps and the Imperial Guards, the elite of the French army and consisting of 140,000 men.

The left of the British line of cantonments reached the great road to Brussels. The right of the Prussian army touched it. On this line it was that Bonaparte designed to penetrate to the capital of the Netherlands thus interposing between the armies of Wellington and Blücher: anticipating their destruction in detail with the consequent revolution and possession of Belgium.

On the 15th the French army cleared the frontiers, moving by the lines of Marchienne and Charleroi.

On the 16th were fought the sanguinary battles of Ligny and Quatre Bras. In both cases the enemy possessed a vast numerical superiority. The 4th Prussian Corps being yet absent, as was the whole of the British cavalry besides a large proportion of artillery and infantry.

Towards the close of the day the front line of the position of Ligny and St. Amant was carried. The mass of the Prussian army retired in the night on Wavre. The extreme left on Sombreffe with the rear of the right on Bree were sustained till the morning of the 17th.

The contest was severe. Some guns which could not be extricated in the night were lost, thus the trophies of the day remained with the enemy.

Marshal Blücher while endeavouring to restore the battle charged at the head of his cavalry and having had his horse shot was for a moment in the power of the enemy. The dusk of evening, however, aided his escape.

The Battle of Quatre Bras terminated differently: the enemy was repulsed at all points with immense slaughter and being in the evening obliged to assume the defensive could with difficulty maintain the position of Frasne. It was on this day that the Duke of Brunswick fell.

On the 17th, Marshal Grouchy(1) with about 20,000 men followed up the Prussians on Wavre, whilst the main body moved on Quatre Bras.

The Duke of Wellington's army, now nearly concentrated, was in a state to advance. The ensemble of the operations, however, requiring a corresponding movement with that of the Prussians, it retired in the afternoon of this day into the position of Mont St Jean or Waterloo.

The operation, masked and executed in good order, was covered by the British cavalry under the Earl of Uxbridge with great gallantry.

The British and Prussian armies covered Brussels, distant twelve miles and, being within a few hours march of each other, could afford mutual cooperation.

In this sketch the Allied forces under the Duke of Wellington are termed for distinction's sake "The British Army". It amounted in position to about 65,000 men of which 9,000 were cavalry with a train of artillery of 150 pieces.

Two thirds of this force consisted of excellent troops, the remainder being new levies and that part raised in the Netherlands of very doubtful loyalty.

The French Army consisted of 110,000 men of which 15,000 were cavalry with 300 pieces of artillery. It was composed of veterans enthusiastic in the cause for which they fought and stimulated at once by the suggestion of interest, a conviction of treason and the recollection of victories.

The position of Waterloo is an elevation of ground which crosses rectangularly near their junction the roads from Nivelles and Charleroi to Brussels.

The line occupied did not exceed one and a half miles: one of the most concentrated dispositions of battle known in modern warfare. A sort of valley from six to eight hundred paces in breadth reached along the front on both sides of the most easy and gradual ascent, terminated by the heights of La Belle Alliance in the brow of which were formed those tremendous batteries pouring forth destruction for hours and covering those solid masses of attack so often pressed forward to the charge and so often driven back by the British.

The ground was in cultivation and quite enclosed, but from the torrents of rain which had fallen, very heavy for the movement of troops.

The Dutch, Flemish, Brunswick, Nassaus, Hanoverian and British forces were organised together, so that a proportion of brigades from each formed a Corps d'armée.

The 1st Corps consisting of the 1st and 3rd British Division, 2nd and 3rd Netherland Divisions and Brunswick Corps. This under the Prince of Orange formed the centre, the right of which rested on the Nivelles road in rear of the farm of Hougoumont, the left on the Charleroi road in rear of La Haye Sainte.

The Reserve consisted of the 5th and 6th British Divisions and a brigade of Belgians attached from the 1st Corps.

Only one brigade of the 6th Division under Major-General Lambert joined during the action, the rest had not yet arrived.

Sir Thomas Picton commanded the Reserve. He occupied the left of the position, the right of which communicated with the left of the centre while a part of the 2nd Corps under Lord Hill formed the right, thrown back from the right of the centre "en potence" and occupying Merke Braine and Braine l'Aleud for the security of that flank.

The 2nd Corps consisted of the 2nd and 4th Divisions and 1st Netherland Division of the 4th Division was present, the rest being at Halle for the security of that line.

A few cavalry were in observation on the high ground to the right of Hougoumont [and] a Brigade of Light Dragoons extended to the left towards La Haye, the remainder of the cavalry being in reserve in rear of the left and centre. The artillery was advanced along the line to the brow of the ridge.

The morning of the 18th threatened a continuance of bad weather. The French who had already anticipated the flight and re-embarkation of the British Army are said to have been at once surprised and delighted to find it still in position; while the latter, confident of the result, with calmness waited the onset.

The soldiers, forgetting the severity of the preceding night, were seen very busily employed in drying their muskets. The note of preparation resounded on all sides.

The day cleared up. The enemy's columns appeared forming on the opposite heights. The troops stood to their arms and skirmishing began along the line. Cannon fire gradually opened till it became an incessant roar.

At noon the Corps of Jerome Bonaparte discovered itself moving in several columns on Hougoumont covered by a heavy discharge of artillery.

1st King's Dragoon Guards private in the uniform worn at Waterloo, except that overalls were worn on service instead of breeches and jackboots.

The farm of Hougoumont occupied by the English Guards under Colonels McDonnell and Horne was the key of that part of the position. A few shrapnel shells well directed, piercing the heads of some of those columns, threw them in disorder. They fell back under cover of a swell of ground, reformed and again pushed forward to attack. This point was disputed with a firmness equivalent to the object and did honour to the defence. It was soon nearly surrounded by the enemy's troops. The enclosure of the garden and the orchard became the scene of a sanguinary conflict: fresh troops continually replacing those fatigued or appalled by the obstinacy of the contest. The enemy succeeded at last by reiterated attacks in penetrating the enclosures. The struggle was long and bloody. The Guards retreated into the house and offices, the walls of which were loop holed[(2)]. Here the contest was maintained with various success and unabated fury: still the enemy (repeatedly forcing this barrier, but always driven out by the bayonet) made no impression and then resorting to shells part of the building caught fire and the flames spread with rapidity. The scene became terrific. In the occasional intermissions of smoke and fire the men were seen fighting hand to hand. In some parts of this dreadful encounter the dead the dying and the wounded, friends and foes intermingled, sunk consumed in the flames.

The post was reinforced and the Guards quickly recovered the enclosures. The enemy fell back dismayed by the failure of so many efforts but continually renewed the attack (tho' with inferior force) throughout the day with the same ill success; with no other result than mutual carnage.

While these operations at Hougoumont lasted, movements of troops were observed in front of our left and centre. The unevenness of the ground concealed the formation of columns but the glittering of bayonets was distinguished at intervals above the small rising grounds. Simultaneous attacks were organised, one of cavalry against the centre, the other of infantry against the left of the British lines. The former

An officer of the 1st King's Dragoon Guards. A French artist's impression painted during the occupation by J. Duplessi Bertaux c.1816, and published in Paris.

came on with all the impetuous fury and audacity displayed by them during all that day. Charging the batteries which lined the brow of the plateau they were met in full onset by the Household Brigade consisting of the Life Guards, Blues and 1st Dragoons under Lord Edward Somerset. Completely overthrown and driven in confusion into the centre of the French line, nothing could surpass the imposing effect of this affair, this shock to the finest cavalry in Europe was executed with rapidity and decision. The clashing of swords and armour resounded through the field and the ground as they fled was covered with wounded and dismounted cuirassiers.

In the meantime an attack on our left was going on by the 1st Corps under Count d'Erlon which consisted of 20,000 men. Infantry in contiguous close columns of 3 or 4,000 [were] each covered by a battery of more than a hundred pieces playing on that part of our line. In this order of battle they suddenly appeared on the opposite heights, instantly rushing forward and with such rapidity that hardly seeming to cross the valley they had already ascended the position and penetrated the British lines.

The 5th Division under Sir T. Picton, Sir James Kempt and Sir Denis Pack lined the crest of the heights with a brigade of Belgians about 40 paces in front and the British brigade of heavy cavalry, viz the Royals, Scots Greys, Enniskillens under Sir W. Ponsonby at an equal distance in the rear.

The Belgians being overthrown in a moment, the enemy advancing with admirable resolution and appearing not at all shaken by a shower of grape and musketry presently crowned the summit. Those parts of our line immediately opposed to them became unavoidably broken: here individuals and small parts were seen to rush sword in hand into the centre and flanks of these immense bodies nobly sustaining even in momentary defeat the honour of their country.

The enemy fatigued and out of breath made no attempt to deploy. The heavy cavalry though not twenty paces distant [was] still nearly masked by the smoke and its situation in the inner declivity, [and] now charged in line. The shock was irresistible: the firing at this point ceased: the smoke cleared off [and] those masses a moment before menacing and conspicious, on whom all eyes were turned, disappeared or left only traces of a dispersed multitude flying over the plain. Vast numbers unable to escape our cavalry now abandoned their arms and threw themselves on the ground. The slope of the position appeared literally covered with the dead. The suddenness of the overthrow worked indescribable confusion, crowds of the enemy were seen surrendering themselves while others, hardly knowing what they did after being rode over by the Dragoons, got up, fired their pieces, flung them down and ran away.

Our cavalry, animated by this success, was broken in advance and could not be reformed; pressing its advantage too far [it] crossed the valley, carried a battery and went through the French line.

The enemy saw the weakness and want of support of this small body and, recovering from the panic which had seized the whole wing, fell upon it with fresh troops and it was not without great difficulty and severe loss that our corps extricated itself.

In this onset Sir Thomas Picton fell in the thickest part of the battle at the head of his troops. This charge cost also the loss of Sir William Ponsonby.

These attacks simultaneous as already observed, on the left and centre, were the second grand effort of Bonaparte and in them he lost at least 15,000 men, dispersed without arms or out of action, and two Eagles, one of which belonged to the regiment once called the "Invincibles" and 2,000 prisoners.

The day growing far advanced Bonaparte, failing on both wings, now resolved to bend all his force against the centre and moved down a strong body of infantry on La Haye Sainte. This point held by a battalion of Hanoverian Jagers(3) was disputed, notwithstanding the immense disparity of numbers, with determined obstinacy. At length the walls were breached in every part and the interior exposed throughout to the fire of grape [sic] and musketry as well as the splinters of the building. A great part of the troops were out of action with all their ammunition expended; most of the rest perished. The enemy having gained possession of the entrance of La Haye Sainte prevented all succour reaching the few troops within it.

Before and during the latter affair a succession of charges were executed along the centre by regiments or brigades of cavalry without combination and less apparently the result of plan than the impetuosity or emulation of some particular corps or commander.

The whole army then formed squares of battalions, reserving their fire with admirable steadiness till the enemy approached close.

The battalions along the brow were repeatedly carried by the enemy but at each retreat [were] reoccupied by our artillery, while soldiers in square, exposed at once to the furious but unavailing assaults of the enemy's cavalry and the dreadful havoc of their artillery, were seen closing their ranks over dead bodies and suffering no other effect than a gradual diminution of front. So dense was the smoke that the noise of arms was often heard before the enemy showed themselves.

Following up their success at La Haye Sainte, heavy columns of infantry were observed continually moving to that point, sheltered by which they endeavoured to renew their formations. Their attacks of cavalry became every moment more serious, large bodies coming down in support. The infantry at the same time were brought up to the brow of the plateau while the fire of all arms continued with tremendous execution. Dragoons, Lancers now came on in masses with unequalled boldness threatening to overwhelm everything at once masking sometimes in line the advance of infantry: again carrying the batteries: rushing with inconceivable force on the immoveable squares [and] pouring through the vacancies of our line even beyond the rear receiving as they passed vollies of musketry then halting in range of our fire confounded by repulse, suffering whole ranks to be mown down by our close unerring discharge [leaving the ground covered with men and horses and charging repeatedly] over their own dead and wounded: at other times anxiously wheeling round our battalions to find an opening, while small parties urged on by a blind fury often pressed forward to seize an unfurled standard and were hewn to pieces at the muzzles of our guns.

In this manner was the battle carried out till nearly the whole of the French cavalry was annihilated.

A corps of infantry succeeded in gaining the level of the plateau just above La Haye Sainte forcing a part of the third division, chiefly Hanoverian Landwher to recoil in disorder. These, however, being rallied by the Duke of Wellington in person, threw themselves into the sunken bye-road or formed a line along it and re-opening their fire effectually checked the advantage.

The British army was seriously diminished and hardly mustered troops enough to line the positions and those so exhausted by their continued exertions as to render the possibility of keeping our ground much longer a subject of anxious consideration.

On the other hand the French infantry who had slowly moved on towards the position, preferring apparently the effect of our fire to that of our bayonets, grew at length appalled by that firing as at the impregnable front of the infantry.

The attacks seemed to relax; the general fire of musketry was confined to skirmishing parties, who persevered with unabated vivacity entrenching themselves often behind the bodies of their own dead or wounded.

It was now about half-past seven p.m. when the Prussians appeared on the field menacing the enemy's right, rear and communications.

Bonaparte, mad with such repeated failures, resolved on a last and desperate effort. The whole of his reserve was ordered to the front, consisting of the Imperial Guards who formed in continguous colums of regiments, supported by the remains of their once formidable cavalry.

By simultaneous attacks on either flank with heavy columns of infantry of the line and by the fire of a battery of 200 pieces they advanced against the centre of the British line.

Bonaparte addressed the troops as they passed and Marshal Ney[5] put himself at their head stirring all that enthusiasm which on similar occasions had so often shown. These celebrated bands accustomed hitherto to decide the fortunes of a battle obeyed this last call with their characteristic boldness: the fury of the struggle was renewed [and] all stood committed to this effort.

The assailants literally marched over heaps of dead bodies. In spirit the contest seemed only to have just begun. It was the struggle however of despair, for the wavering of the enemy line showed the dismay which began to pervade the disappointed columns. While our front kept their original ground the decisive moment now came and the Duke made his final dispositions. The squares successively wheeled into line: a brigade of cavalry under General Vivian moved from Hougoumont on the French rear. The Light Infantry Brigade under General Adams with others of the right wing had been brought up "en potence"[6] to support the centre during the previous attacks on that part of the line. This brigade now thrust forward the right shoulder, presenting an oblique front to the enemy's left flank [and] at the same time forming an angle with the 1st British Brigade under General Maitland, directly opposed to the Imperial Guard. On the plateau yet further to the left was concentrated in columns the main body of the British cavalry, headed by the remains of the Heavy and Household Brigade and led by the Earl of Uxbridge.

In this order of battle the word was given to advance. The order ran like lightning along the line. The cavalry from every quarter rushed on the advance columns. The firing now ceased, all was clear to the sight and the sun, hitherto rather clouded, shone with peculiar force.

The formation of the enemy's lines and columns could hardly be traced. In some places they presented a front, in others nothing was seen but huge masses recoiling and driving back their own ranks.

The artillery were hurrying to the roads which in their confusion they soon jammed up. Presently all appearance of order was lost and this immense army, cuirassiers, dragoons, infantry of the line, the Imperial Guards, all who so lately were so formidable to oppose, were now flying in one ungovernable heap. Officers and men, each seemingly mindful of his own safety regardless, trampled over the unfortunate who fell, contributing to complete the horrible work of destruction which began to rage with indescribable fury. The Allied Squadrons, but particularly the Prussians, fell on their flanks and rear as if to quench their thirst with blood. No respite or quarter was given while their strength remained to follow up their vengeance. It became afterwards a subject of astonishment how the enemy could find power to escape so fast. The dispersion was so great that Marshal Ney himself stated that for three days he saw not even an orderly near him.

The British Army bivouacked on the heights of La Belle Alliance. The Prussians continued the pursuit all night.

(1) Maréchal Emmanuel, Marquis de Grouchy (1766-1847) was born into a noble family and joined the French artillery and then the cavalry before becoming an officer of the King's Bodyguard (Gardes du Corps du Roi). He espoused the cause of the French Revolution but was obliged to resign his commission as a member of the Revolutionary forces because of his noble background. Back in the army in 1794, he fought in many campaigns and in 1815 rallied to Napoleon on his return from exile. He was given command of the cavalry reserve of the Army of the North in June 1815 and was then transferred to command the right wing. His refusal to march towards the sound of cannon at Waterloo – he insisted instead on carrying out his latest orders to the letter – led Napoleon to blame him for the outcome. His skills as a cavalry commander have been widely praised but as a human being his character was flawed in many respects, as he often changed allegiances when circumstances made it expedient for him to do so.

(2) Loop-holed. A loop-hole was a small gap or hole in a wall – especially a fortified wall. It came into colloquial use as a flaw or way out of a problem ("find the loop-hole").

(3) Jagers. A Jäeger was a marksman in certain units of the German or Austrian armies and the name has its origin in the German word "Jäger" or hunter.

(4) Landwher. Mis-spelling for Landwehr or ground forces.

(5) Maréchal Michel Ney (1769-1815) had a distinguished military career and played an important role in many of Napoleon's successes. He was nicknamed 'bravest of the brave' after his exploits in Russia and was reputedly the last Frenchman to leave that country. In 1814 he became spokesman for the Marshals demanding Napoleon's abdication and was in high favour with the Bourbons at the beginning of 1815. However, when Napoleon returned to France, Ney rejoined him at Auxerre. He was appointed Battle Commander at Waterloo and some say that his mishandling of the infantry and cavalry attacks led to the French defeat. The Bourbons had him arrested when he returned to Paris and he was executed by firing squad on 7 December 1815.

(6) "En potence" – a military support manoeuvre described in Chapter IX. From the French word meaning a crutch.

Prussian soldiers

CHAPTER FIVE

A Summary of the positions occupied by the various allied units engaged and an Analysis of the Battle of Waterloo into four different attacks by the French. Undated.

This anonymous, undated account is a battlefield guide showing the positions of the various units engaged.

The following remarks, with the Duke of Wellington's despatch and the French account of the Battle of Waterloo, may assist to give a tolerable idea of events.

From the village of Mont St. Jean go along the Genappe Chaussée until you arrive at a single tree on the right of the road, to which they have given the name of the Duke of Wellington's Tree, as he frequently stood near it during the battle. At this tree, cross roads branch off to the right and left, the former leading towards Hougoumont, the latter to the village of La Haye. Take the cross road to the right it will take you to the ridge which was occupied by the 1st and 2nd Divisions. Following this road you will arrive at three trees at the termination of the ridge. The right of the 1st Division rested at this ridge and the left of the 3rd Division rested on the Genappe Chaussée near the single tree. On the ground between these two points the squares of those divisions resisted the repeated attacks of cavalry and afterwards (being formed in alternate squares and lines of four deep) repulsed the Imperial Guard.

From the three trees you descend to Hougoumont. The house and garden of Hougoumont we kept during the day. The French for a time had possession of the orchard on the left of the garden and the wood in front of it.

From Hougoumont cross over to Belle Alliance. Here you will be shown the hill on which Bonaparte is said to have been during the greater part of the day and from which you will have a good view of our position.

From Belle Alliance follow the cross road leading from thence to the village of La Haye for about two hundred yards when you will meet with a track on your left made by the enemy's artillery in moving to attack Sir Thomas Picton's division posted on Mont St. Jean. By following this track which perhaps is still visible you will perceive [how] the enemy, in order to conceal this movement and keep clear of the fire of the artillery, followed the course of the ravines and suddenly appeared on the height within about four hundred yards of the position occupied by Sir T. Picton's division. When his artillery opened his columns rushed to the attack.

Sir T. Picton's division was formed in rear of the cross road leading to the village of La Haye which branches from the chaussée at the single tree. His right rested on the chaussée and his left on the highest point of Mont St. Jean. There is a small wood in rear and rather to the left of the place the left of this division stood.

The Belgian and Dutch troops were in reserve, part in rear of the left of the 3rd Division and the remainder behind Sir T. Picton's left, occupying also the village of La Haye.

You must next see the farm of La Haye Sainte which was taken and retaken during the day.

From the height above Hougoumont (at the three trees), you will see the ground occupied by Lord Hill's corps. The right on Braine l'Alleud and the left on the Nivelles chaussée.

General Adam's brigade, the 51st, 71st and a battalion of the 95th were brought up from Lord Hill's corps in the latter part of the day to fill up the interval caused by detaching nearly the whole of the 2nd Brigade of Foot Guards to the support of Hougoumont. Generals Grant, Vandeleur and Dornberg's[(1)] brigades of cavalry were placed in the hollow in the rear of the 1st and 3rd Divisions and came up to meet the attacks made by the French cavalry on those divisions.

The Household Brigade (Lord Edward Somerset) was on the right and left of the Genappe chaussée near the farm of Mont St. Jean; General Ponsonby's Brigade in rear of Sir T. Picton and Vivian's Brigade on the left of the whole.

The battle may be divided into four attacks:

1st. The attack on Hougoumont which began about noon and was sustained during the whole day though only faintly after three o'clock.

2nd. The attack on Sir T. Picton which began about half past one.

3rd. The general attack of the enemy's cavalry which began between four and five o'clock.

Lastly, the attack of the Imperial Guard which succeeded the attacks of cavalry and continued till near eight o'clock at which hour we turned the tables by a general attack on them.

---

(1) Generals Grant and Vandeleur. General Sir Colquhoun Grant (1765-1835) commanded a Hussar brigade at Waterloo. He was promoted to Lieutenant General in 1830. General Sir John Ormsby Vandeleur (1763-1849) commanded the 4th Cavalry Brigade at Waterloo and was promoted General in 1838.

CHAPTER SIX

A series of letters to Ben Sydenham from his brother Thomas from Brussels and Paris. 5 July – 11 August 1815

This chapter, a series of letters between 5th July – 11th August, 1815, from Thomas Sydenham to his brother Benjamin, gives first the numbers engaged during the Waterloo campaign. The chief interest however lies in the description of the state of France, and more particularly of Paris, immediately after the occupation by the Allies. It gives an amusing account of the ridicule in which the unfortunate Louis XVIII was held even in a respectable quarter of the city.

The aloof attitude of the Duke of Wellington to the political situation and the writer's opinion of the statesmen involved are of particular interest in view of the inside knowledge which Thomas Sydenham, due to his connections, was able to obtain.

Wellington's appreciation of Napoleon is dealt with by the Editor but the Duke's own comments on the Battle of Waterloo give an insight into this man's true character as does a more intimate incident which Thomas describes.

Brussels, 5th July, 1815.

My dear Ben,

Since you left us we have received intelligence from authority which would justify my quitting Brussels for Paris: however, the King of France has invited the Prince de Condé to go to Cambrai(1) and he consequently leaves Brussels tomorrow morning with fifty-two gentlemen with hooked noses, bald heads, thin tails, and little bits of red ribbon! It is a glorious show!

I saw Fitzroy Somerset both yesterday and this morning and we have had as much conversation as the pain of his arm will allow. He gave me a clear and detailed account of the battle from its commencement until six thirty pm when he was carried from the field and I was able to understand the relation perfectly from having looked at the ground the day before.

The effective strength of Lord Wellington's army before the operations was 75,000 men, viz:

British and German infantry		23,000
Cavalry		9,000
		32,000
Hanoverians	11,000	
Dutch and Belgian infantry	22,000	
Brunswickers	7,000	
Estoff's Cavalry	950	40,950
		72,950
Besides these there were two battalions of Nassauer troops about		1,500
		74,450

Of these troops the German Legion and the British were the only part on whom complete reliance could be placed. The Hanoverians fine men, but undisciplined and unaccustomed to service and badly officered. The Dutch and Belgians very bad. The Brunswickers tolerably good while they had their Prince at their head. The New Nassauers showed no qualities but speed in retreat and great respect for cannon balls.

But of the 76,950 men only 50,000 were brought into action. We lost 4,000 in the affair of the 16th (June). Estoff's cavalry had not joined. Prince Frederick of Orange with 11,000 Dutch and Belgians was in position at Halle, 2 brigades of Colville's(2) Division (4,500) were at Braine le Compte, a division of Dutch and Belgians (6,000) were in position at Braine l'Alleud to watch our extreme right and they had not occasion to fire a shot. Many Dutch took the liberty of retiring on the 17th (June) having seen enough the day preceding. The effective strength of Blücher's army before the operations of the 16th did not exceed 100,000 men. They had 15,000 placed hors de combat on the 16th so that the whole strength of the allies in the field on the morning of the 18th amounted to 135,000 of all arms. The strength of Bonaparte's army amounted to about 110,000 infantry and 22,000 cavalry with 450 pieces (of artillery).

The loss of the British and German legion amounts to 750 officers and about 11,000 privates.

8th July

I heard yesterday from Fitzroy Somerset that Lord Wellington had concluded a military convention with the Commander-in-Chief of the French Army by which the allies are to have possession of Paris, and the French Army is to retire beyond the Loire. This has determined me to proceed on to Paris and I shall leave Brussels tomorrow for that purpose (Sunday 9th). Conway remains here till Monday and intends to pass some days at St. Quentin on his road. I shall be at Mons on the 9th, Cambrai on the 10th, Roye on the 11th, Senlis on the 12th, Paris on the 13th, etc. etc. etc. - TS

Paris, Saturday, 15th July, 1815.

I continue to write though I write in pain and have not much to communicate. I spent yesterday evening tête-a-tête with Sir Charles Stuart. The aspect of affairs has considerably improved since the morning. The submission of the Army of the Loire, the surrender of Lille, Mauberge and Verdun and the restoration of tranquility at Lyons and Dijon put the King almost in complete possession of France.

Nothing of consequence now remains except Strasbourg where there are 30,000 French troops blockaded by 70,000 allies, but it is generally thought the former will follow the example of their comrades on the Loire and submit to the Royal government.

I don't think the government has received any despatches of what has taken place at Toulon(3), but on the whole it may fairly be asserted that Louis' authority is fully recognised and established throughout the whole of his dominions. It is said that he intends to profit by his late experience and to adapt measures to prevent the recurrence of those circumstances by which he was so tamely expelled from the throne.

The dismissal of Blacas and admission of Fouché(4) into the ministry is a strong proof of his determination to sacrifice his personal feelings to the interest and safety of his government, for his affection and esteem for Blacas were very sincere: his aversion to Fouché deep rooted and was supposed to be insurmountable.

The scene of crying and embracing which took place between the King and Blacas on the latter finally retiring was quite infantile. His Majesty has repeatedly declared his fixed resolution never to admit Fouché to his confidence or to any situation either in the Cabinet or about his person: it is said to be the King's intention to dissolve the present army and to reform it from top to bottom [and] to raise a strong guard for the protection of his person, selecting proper men from the infantry, cavalry and artillery of the army instead of the old "Maison du Roi". The whole of the guard would be stationed in and about Paris near his person.

I have no doubt that the King's authority will be perfectly secure as long as the Allies remain in Paris or on the frontiers, but when the whole business shall have been settled and everyone returned peaceably to his own home we shall then have to observe whether the Royal Authority in the hands of the present King, at the head of such a family and in the midst of such a court, will be sufficiently respected and capable of maintaining itself.

The Congress for the general settlement of affairs has already commenced its deliberations and meets every day at the hotel of the English ambassador. This Congress, or rather committee, consists of the Prime Ministers of the four great powers viz:- Metternich (Austria), Nesselrode (Russia), Hardenberg (Prussia), Castlereagh (Britain). None of our Ambassadors at the foreign courts or those of the other powers assist at the deliberations. The Padrone is, of course, admitted but I think he affects to avoid interference in political business; to confine himself to the duties of his profession and to speak rather contemptuously of diplomacy, politics, statesmen, etc. etc.

On leaving Stuart's room last night I met the whole of the Committee coming down stairs with the addition of Pozzo de Borgho. The Padrone took me aside and we walked for sometime together up and down the street; he enquired very kindly after you and then talked about Lord Wellesley. He was very anxious to know the state of his pecuniary concerns and whether any arrangement would still be made to save him from ultimate embarrassment. But my information on this was very slender but I believed some arrangement was either in contemplation or progress by which he would be relieved from all his present difficulties and have a clear and comfortable income for the future. He seemed much pleased to hear this and said if Wellesley had a sufficient income for a gentleman to live comfortably his friends ought to be very indifferent as to his coming into office. We had then some talk about the Battle and subsequent military operations. I asked him what he now thought of Bonaparte as a General and whether the result of the late operations had raised or lowered his opinion of Bonaparte's military talents. He said his opinion of Bonaparte remained unchanged, that there was nothing very rare or extraordinary in him as a General: that he always thought him a great glutton, fighting very hard to carry a particular point, but showing no resource if his main attack failed: that at the Battle of Waterloo he kept driving at the two villages and the ground between them as long as he could get his troops to advance to the attack: that in all this there was very little manoeuvering and nothing of what would formerly be called great generalship, either in the conception of the plan or in the execution of it. I asked him if he thought him very different from a superior to his Marshals. He said No. It appeared to him to be very much the same sort of thing.

I observed that in talking about the Battle of Waterloo he invariable mentioned it with some expression of horror, such as, "it was a tremendous affair". "It was a terrible battle", or, "it was a dreadful day", holding up his arms above his head and shaking his hands. He repeatedly said he never had taken so much pains about a battle, that no battle had ever cost him so much terrible anxiety [and] that he owed the victory entirely to the admirable conduct of the old Spanish infantry (meaning the regiments which had served under him in Spain), which he says he is certain is the best infantry in the world: that the other English regiments, though they behaved tolerably well, yet often in the course of the day shuffled, got unsteady and alarmed and that it required great exertions to keep them together. As for all the rest of the troops they repeatedly gave way and would have left the field altogether if they had not had an infantry to rally under.

I asked him how the French troops had behaved. He merely said their cavalry was very bold. Fitzroy Somerset, however, assured me that during the whole day the French infantry *fought very shy* and were on almost every occasion repulsed by the fire of our artillery.

I asked the Padrone what had led to the sudden and general extinction of the French army. He said that, a general attack on the left of his line having entirely failed, the enemy retired with great precipitation and in much disorder. Soon after this he observed the fire of Bülow's(5) columns advancing rapidly on the flank and rear of the enemy. He then saw he could attack the enemy with certain success and immediately ordered the whole line to advance and though the troops had been fighting since morning and consequently were much fatigued, yet the order to advance was received with general acclamation [and] they stepped forward with wonderful alacrity.

He told me Lord Uxbridge was rather alarmed at this forward movement and particularly advised [him] not to advance beyond the range of heights occupied originally by the French (where you may recollect to have seen the telegraph). The Padrone directly answered "Oh damn it! in for a penny, in for a pound is my maxim and if the troops advance they shall go as far as they can". A few moments after this Lord Uxbridge was wounded.

All was now disorder in the French army and whole battalions threw down their arms and ran across the fields. He says from the accounts he received since he reached Paris, he is convinced the French lost 100,000 men by the Battle of Waterloo in killed, wounded, prisoners and dispersion; in short in men who would never had joined their colours again during the present war.

11th August.

The Padrone called upon me this morning and though he was wet through he stayed near an hour. It is very difficult drawing any opinion from him of the state of affairs in France, although he seems desirous of receiving those of others. I told him I thought the prospect very gloomy and dark, that I thought the Royalists though numerous were weak, that their enemies were bold, active, enterprising and great rascals in general; that excepting the King, the rest of the Bourbons were hated and despised and I showed him by a ridiculous anecdote that even the King's person was not spared by the wits of Paris. I observed that there was an extinction of all sound principle, of all moral sentiment and of all public and political principle in France: that there was no attachment either to any person, or to any family, or to any form of government: that when the minds of a whole nation were let loose in this way or rendered callous or indifferent by the frequency of changes and a succession of sufferings it was in vain to get a base on which to erect a foundation of any family or form of government: that in this way despotism was the only remedy.

It was impossible for any government to be strong, efficient or durable without immense authority, power almost unlimited, and the decided employment of it. That I considered France now to be as imperfectly governed as any part of Persia or India. This, as nearly as I can recollect, the substance of what I said. He listened with deep attention and agreed to every conclusion. Before going away he said "I believe it is all very bad".

There is a great miracle taken place at Paris, everybody praises the Emperor Alexander(6). They all say he has acted with wisdom, moderation, and discretion which do him honour. He had made his court so effectually to the Hereditary Prince of Orange that he has drawn H.S.H. entirely from the Duke and the Prince's only companions now are Czernichoff and the Emperor's favourite equerries and Aide-de-Camps. Alava abuses the Prince roundly and tells me he is not at all the same person I remember in Spain.

After the Battle of Waterloo the Prince in a proud fit said to Alava triumphantly "Well, Miguel what should we have done if we had had the Carrajos with us?". Alava answered "About the same we have done now with the difference that the Spaniards would not have run away till the firing had commenced, but the Dutch and Belgians did not wait for that signal before they began their flight".

The anecdote about Louis XVIII which I related to the Padrone, was that in the Boulevards here in my neighbourhood a few nights ago, the canaille dressed up a large hog like the King of France with his Chapeau plume, St. Esprit Cordon Bleu and Manteau selon les règles. They conduct His Majesty in great pomp up the Boulevards shouting "Vive le roi, vive notre aimable roi, vive le desiré" and singing "Henri Quatre" and other royal songs. By the time the hog reached the first corps de garde the officer asked what this meant for he could not see H.M. The crowd said "we are parading about an effigy of our good king. Look sir how this resembles him; the same expression of kindness, the same figure and the same graces". The officer, an animal and a bigger pig than the one representing the King took it all exactly on its face value and turned out the guard.

This farce lasted two hours before it was detected by the police and the crowd dispersed. Then this poor pig was let loose, kicked, buffeted and pursued to his home again. And yet we consider ourselves as composing one of the most loyal quarters of Paris.

There cannot be much foundation for the report of legal proceedings which you allude to for the gentleman and lady dined at his Grace's the day before yesterday and his Grace was parading about the lady in the evening while the gentleman was endeavouring to prove to Stuart that according to the dignity and rank of their profession, Lord Byron qua Poet was a greater man than the Duke of Wellington qua general and that Childe Harold would be read when nobody would think of Waterloo.

Alava says he has now seen all the great statesmen of the Continent and he thinks better of the Spaniards than ever: that he will match Cavallos against Talleyrand, Metternich, Nerselrode, Castlereagh and all the rest in a heap. I told him I thought exactly the same thing of Meer Ali and Nana. He allows that Pozzo de Borgo is a man of superior calibre.

etc. ect. etc. T.S.

---

(1) Cambrai. The French armies marched from Cambrai to Villers-en-Cauchies before the battle of that name which took place during the Netherlands campaign on 24 April 1794. A heavily outnumbered force of Allied cavalry was victorious.

(2) Colville's Division was named after General the Hon Sir Charles Colville, Commander of the 4th Division during the siege of Badajoz in 1812.

(3) Siege of Toulon 7 September – 19 December 1793. A very important event in Napoleon's career when his intervention at the age of 24 helped to break the siege of British, Spanish and French emigré troops who were supporting the Bourbon cause. It was the event which first brought him to public notice.

(4) Joseph Fouché, Duc d'Otranto (1759-1820) was one of history's survivors, combining

expediency with thoroughness. He was Napoleon's Minister of Police until 1810 and again during the 100 days.

(5) General Friedrich von Bülow, Count Dennewitz (1755-1816) was a Prussian commander and hero of the War of German Liberation. The arrival of his corps, near Plancenoit on the afternoon of 18 June was a critical event in the battle of Waterloo.

(6) Alexander I, Tsar of Russia (1777-1825) succeeded his father Paul I in 1801. In April 1805, he joined the Third Coalition (of Russia, Great Britain, Austria and Sweden with some German Princes). After the Russian and Austrian armies were defeated at Austerlitz in December 1805, he made peace with Napoleon at Tilsit in 1807, joining the Continental System and declaring war on Great Britain. After 1809, relations between Russia and France deteriorated largely because of economic reasons. Alexander's decision to open his ports to British trade led to Napoleon's invasion of Russia. Alexander refused to treat with Napoleon even after the fall of Moscow. After the Congress of Vienna in 1815 Alexander hoped, through a "holy alliance" with Austria and Prussia to establish a new Christian order in Europe. In later years, he became something of a mystic.

Life Guards

CHAPTER SEVEN

A letter from Captain GA Barlow to his Father Written in Paris 7 July 1815 about his experiences in the Waterloo Campaign

This account of the battle is of considerable interest for two reasons: first because it was written by a comparatively junior officer and second because he was a very observant young man.

Besides his own somewhat hair-raising experiences he took the trouble to co-relate them as far as he could with what had happened in "another part of the field". He admits that his view of the campaign was localised by his own circumstances which is more than many eye-witness accounts of battles do.

According to the Waterloo Roll Call, the only Barlow present at the battle was George Ulrich of the 69th Foot (later 2nd Bn. The Welch Regiment). This is borne out by the text of his letter. He was the eldest son of Sir George Barlow Bart. of Fort William, Bengal (Calcutta) and he exchanged into the 4th Light Dragoons in 1821.

Barlow died in India in 1824 and his widow married William, Earl Nelson.

Once more there is an error in the transcription of the last initial.

Captain GA Barlow to his father.

Camp near Paris
July 7th, 1815.

My dear Father,

Since the few hasty lines written to you at sunrise on the 19th June, I have scarcely had an hour to call my own. Excepting the 23rd we have been making daily forced marches and these rapid strides brought us on the 1st July in sight of the great city.

I have moreover been of late protempore acting as Brigade Major and undertook it at a moment of no ordinary difficulty, when the loss of every adjutant but one, most of the sergeant majors and the absence of all the regimental books rendered it rather a troublesome office.

The decisiveness of the blow struck on the 18th ultimo is best provided by our rapid progress thus far. The march has appeared more like a triumphal procession than an invasion of a hostile country. A shot has been scarcely fired since the affair of La Belle Alliance and here we are encamped in the Bois de Boulogne.

I will as briefly as possible recapitulate the principal occurrences since the campaign opened.

We left Soignies on the 16th June and marched to Nivelles in the direction of Fleurus. Bonaparte having concentrated his army at Mauberge on the 14th entered Belgium and drove the Prussians from Charleroi. On the 15th Marshal Blücher resolved to give him battle on the 16th (June) although a large corps of his army under Bülow was not yet arrived. This took place at Fleurus and the Prussians after a very gallant contest against superior numbers being worsted were obliged to retire with severe loss in men and cannon. As I said before we moved from Soignies on the same day to their succour but when we reached Nivelles we found there was work enough for ourselves.

Marshal Ney had penetrated within a league of that town. Our division (General Altens) hastened forward and found General Picton's division with some Belgic troops engaged against disproportionate forces which our reinforcement by no means made equal. It was a fine summer's evening, about five o'clock, when we first came into fire and we were soon in a heavy cannonade.

The division was then formed into squares of regiments, a measure which the enemy's cavalry being close upon us and our own total want of that kind of force rendered absolutely necessary.

The scene of action was a ground diversified with little dales and gently rising slopes, covered throughout with rye and wheat which here grew five or six feet high.

In course of manouevering the 69th for a moment found itself at the bottom of one of these little dips and being formed in square was quite secure. A certain personage who shall be nameless sent down a message that the 69th should deploy into line. The order was obeyed but scarcely done when a strong body of French cuirassiers, as if by magic, showed themselves close in rear of our flank about fifty yards off. I have said we happened to be in a small hollow and the height of the surrounding corn precluded the view of anything beyond that distance.

The enemy, taking advantage of this, approached close to the Regiment quite unperceived and rushed out as from an ambuscade on the flank of the line. We were absolutely defenceless: an attempt was made to form square but the cuirassiers by their instantaneous attack rendered it impossible: in a word they rode through and over our little Battalion of 4,000 men (sic): one colour was taken in the confusion which ensured the other was preserved. Many of our unfortunate men were sabred and wounded but no prisoners made as the neighbouring regiments, taking warning by us, quickly threw themselves into squares and before the cuirassiers could form again they kept up such a terrible fire that the greater part of our gallant enemy fell on the spot.

Night coming on the whole of the French army retired into an adjoining wood and we bivouacked on the field of battle.

I have been thus circumstantial as the event of losing a standard has been blazoned in the French papers and I have attempted to account for it as a case of misfortune and not of dishonour. Perhaps it was almost unavoidable, my opinion is formed upon a very minute examination of the spot and the circumstances and I dispassionately surveyed the ground.

As for George himself, when he saw the game was up and all resistance useless and some of these armour bearing cavaliers close at his back, he had the presence of mind to throw himself on the ground. The enemy passed by and over him. He had often heard of their "ruse" and being incapable of running he had no other resource left. He waited awhile and then getting on his legs made the best of his way to the square of the 42nd Regiment which saved him. Towards dusk he returned to the spot where he had left his servant and horse.

Upon my arrival I learnt that a Belgic, Brunswick and Foreign Hussar had attacked my poor servant and wounded him so desperately in the arm that it was necessary to amputate it next morning. They took away at the same time my much valued horse Barrosa and I have never since been able to get any tidings of it. The thief probably made direct for Brussels and disposed of his spoil there. Thus was I left destitute for the march and retreat of the following day the 17th. It deprived me also of my cloak and coat to keep off the heaviest rain I ever knew: will you believe I walked on the 17th between thirteen and fourteen miles to the position of Waterloo in crossroads of the most execrable description. The circumstances of the occasion, however, kept me up and I was determined to hold out to the last for towards evening the enemy's cavalry came along the pavée and took many prisoners of those who had straggled or lagged behind the march of the columns.

Night came on and with it the floodgates of heaven seemed to open: it rained in torrents without intermission. We had no covering, nothing to eat and thus hungry, drenched and sleepless around a fire which hardly could be made to burn did we await in a cornfield the dawning of 18th June.

Having before witnessed the system of our great chief, the tendency of all our movements the preceding evening led me to think a general action would ensue the next day for the preservation of Brussels. The Prussians made a corresponding movement in retreat on Wavre and the whole of the English and Hanoverian army during the evening and night of the 17th by various routes and in different columns marched into the position of Waterloo.

Our force as nearly as I can ascertain being rather more than 80,000 men of all sorts and descriptions inclusive of the Prussian division of General Bülow but, of course, not the rest of Marshal Blücher's army.

The position of Waterloo upon which the destinies of Europe were about to be fought is nothing more than a range of moderately rising grounds touching upon the right of the pavée leading from Nivelles to Brussels and extending on the left to the high road from Genappe conducting also to Brussels. These two routes formed the summit of an angle meeting near Braine l'Alleud to which the position of the British

Army served as a base on 3rd side, its flanks leaning upon and thus covering either approach. It was fine, open, commanding, fighting ground but transversable in every direction by cavalry and cannon. The British artillery lined the whole summit of these heights and the army was drawn up in order of battle behind them a little way down the reverse of the hill, so as to be perfectly concealed from the enemy who could by no means get a sight of its force or disposition and, according to their own confession, they were kept ignorant of our intentions. To get the wished for peep behind, it was necessary to come up to the very muzzles of 150 pieces of cannon placed in different directions and some sturdy fellows in the rear.

The French position was of a corresponding nature, parallel to our own: the party quitting its ground therefore laboured under certain disadvantage but which the superiority of the assailants in this case ought, however, to have counterbalanced.

One corps being left to watch the Prussians, Bonaparte brought the remaining four (corps) and the whole of the Imperial Guard (about 20,000) and upwards of 200 guns against the Duke of Wellington's army.

The day became fair about eleven and the cannonade on both sides commenced. An impetuous attack was first made against the right where the Guards and German Legion held some loopholed houses and a small coppice. The Germans quitted their post after an admirable defence, the enemy having set fire to the buildings. The Guards, more fortunate, constantly maintained theirs against repeated attacks and greatly distinguished themselves. Abbatis thrown across the road impeded the enemy much and after many fruitless efforts directed themselves against the centre where General Allen's corps was posted. This happened about two o'clock when our friends the cuirassiers again showed themselves and by the rapidity of their advance forced our artillery men to quit their guns. They galloped away however with the limbers and traces so that the enemy had no means of carrying them off over

'Left Parry', 1st King's Dragoon Guards. From Captain James Naylor's sketchbook.

ploughed grounds. Those on foot took shelter in the squares of infantry which had been formed in that order since the commencement of the attack and were a short distance in rear all perfectly prepared.

The cuirassiers and dragoons then tried to pierce the squares but were received with such a terrible fire that they were thrown into the greatest disorder and obliged to fly with all possible speed. Such was the result of the first attack of cavalry which I had conceived to have been a reconnaissance on the part of the enemy, but to my great surprise this was succeeded by a second on the left, then a third and afterwards by a variety of others during three hours till five o'clock, on every part of this division and Lord Hill's corps.

These attacks were repeated and in the most daring manner. Their officers, I saw, led them on in a very gallant style and their men followed the example but the squares stood firm throughout, not one of them for a moment was in disorder.

The enemy's cavalry repeatedly dashed into the centre of the British position and at every attempt was received with such destructive vollies from the squares as to excite my astonishment at such useless devotion. Nor were they discontinued till the flower of the French cavalry both in men and horses were almost totally destroyed. The remainder could not be brought to act with much effort soon afterwards when their services were most urgently required, as will presently appear.

Between six and seven o'clock Bonaparte ordered forward his infantry and several large masses were put in motion and they began to ascend the British position in various directions, covered by the fire of all his batteries. Our cannon was then ordered to be pointed against these columns. They played with terrible effect so as to retard perpetually their advance. As soon as they reached the proper distance our infantry commenced and after a very heavy fire on both sides we succeeded in making them retire. Eight o'clock came and found the battle yet undecided for shortly afterwards four masses of the Imperial Guard (infantry) advanced and made a most formidable attack. These fellows came up with "carried arms" in the most determined manner to within seventy or eighty yards of the heights along which our infantry were posted and opened a most terrible fire. Two pieces of cannon accompanied them and being opposite our Brigade, then formed "en masse", raked it very severely with grape shot as did the shells from some distant howitzers. This was indeed the crisis of this most eventful day. Both armies were in close contact and hot action in the cannonade really tremendous along the whole line: for the entire artillery of both armies were in full play to support their respective sides in an effort to decide the fortune of the battle.

The sun was now setting very fast and the clouds of smoke from this tremendous firing had so obscured the faint gleams of the declining day that to distinguish friend from foe became extremely embarrassing. Some Dutch infantry on our flank resembling the French in our front so much that I caught several of our men firing at them. Presently I was surprised with a view of the Duke and all his staff close in the rear. He was pointing in various directions and seemingly occupied in explaining some important arrangement. This was soon after found to be an order for a general attack on our part. Cavalry, artillery, infantry all made a simultaneous move and descending the heights advanced towards the enemy who from that moment were thrown into the most frightul disorder.

The British cavalry made a number of brilliant charges cutting through various masses of infantry and taking cannon by the dozen as well as an enormous number of prisoners. From this moment all description would be useless. Everything was a complete heap of confusion as might be expected from the magnitude of such mighty hosts in close pursuit of a flying enemy.

In the morning there were not less than 90,000, most of whom now threw away both arms and knapsacks and sought refuge by flight: for every man it was "sauve qui peut" (let every man look after himself). At this crucial moment, General Bülow's cavalry and artillery arrived and completed the success of the glorious day. They were quite fresh and pursued the enemy throughout the night.

The Duke had already taken in the field 150 pieces of cannon: 7,000 prisoners he sent to Brussels, besides thousands of wounded on the ground and in villages whom humanity hindered our moving. But General Bülow fairly ruined them. He found 60 pieces more and took, I believe, as many prisoners as the British throughout the day. I am afraid to guess how many the Prussians killed and wounded of their enemy as for a long time they gave no quarter. Their co-operation was really most important as it so totally annihilated and dispersed this once formidable army that it never afterwards appeared in a regular and organised body.

These are the principal features of this most decisive day: at least such as come within the limited sphere of my observation. An actor in these scenes is least of all calculated to give a fair or general description of them. Indeed, to do justice to this gallant army and their chief would be no ordinary task. The fate of Europe depended in a great measure on their exertions and so fully sensible was the Duke of the magnitude of the stake that in answer to a question put by someone as to the course of operations to be pursued in the event of any personal accident happening to him, he answered, "fight this position to the last man". Frightful would indeed have been the consequence of defeat on our part. Let people say what they will, I should have been very sorry to have been near any Belgic troops in case of a reverse. The Dutch are exempted from this suspicion but the fidelity of the others was very questionable: that is, they would have sided with the strongest. Bonaparte acknowledged that in Brussels he had many partisans. The city and Ghent would have fallen immediately into his hands, and no resource would have been left to us but a rapid retreat across the Scheldt into Holland.

Flanders being won, Marshal Blücher and his army must have sought safety in Hanover or Saxony. Separated from the British he could not have withstood the superior number of his antagonists. In short, the result would have been perhaps more disastrous than it is now great and advantageous.

Bonaparte is said to have made the greatest exertions. A wounded soldier of the Guard told me he was dressed in a grey coat and at one time was very close to our position. He had gained considerable advantages on the 16th and 17th and was so confident of a similar result on the 18th that many proclamations were found in his baggage dated from the Chateau de Laeken, his old imperial villa, near Brussels.

The Battle of La Belle Alliance has also established a very convincing proof of the superiority of infantry over cavalry, allowing each to have done its best. This was surely exemplified this day. The French cuirassiers charged with a devotion and courage impossible to be surpassed. They rode close up to the squares and passed between them in every direction. They never flinched and never ceased attacking until their losses in horses and men in so many fruitless attempts became so enormous that it would have been madness to have persisted.

The British cavalry in our part of the position were very inferior in numbers to that of the enemy and were therefore frequently obliged to retire behind the squares of infantry, which together with the artillery, stood their ground most steadily. In saying this I do not wish to be understood as casting any reflections on our brethren of the cavalry. What I have already mentioned fully justified their conduct and under more favourable circumstances at the end of the day they highly distinguished themselves.

One fault is allowed by most military men to have been committed by the enemy in the improvident manner of exposing their cavalry. This arm of force was so totally ruined during the early part of the day as to be quite incapable of protecting the retreat of their broken infantry at the close of the afternoon: that of the guard suffered particularly. They were the picked men of the French army. A wounded man told me that Bonaparte on his return from Elba to recruit this corps ordered a certain number of the choicest men from every regiment throughout the service to be sent him. Thus was condensed in one mass the very flower l'elite of the French infantry and with it he did make a most powerful attempt to fix the fortunes of that day: but providence decreed otherwise and that on the heights of St. Jean his abdication should be virtually made although the instrument was executed at Paris a few days later.

Night came on and with it some repose to our wearied frames after the exertions of so arduous a day. At sunrise next morning I penned a few lines to you and then proceeded to pay the last offices to the remains of our poor Colonel and of Captains Hobhouse and Blackwood; my two most intimate friends who fell on the field of honour. This done we took a farewell view of the position of Belle Alliance.

On the 20th to Binch: 21st to Bavay where we entered France: 22nd to Gomminies: 23rd halted: 24th to Boissies: 25th Senain: 26th to Caulaincourt: 27th to the famous plain and village of Crecy: 28th to Boulogne: 29th Houdricourt: 30th to Pontaine (Nr. Senlis): 1st July came in sight of Paris and halted at the little village of Annay about six miles from the barriers, being a march of something more than 180 miles since the morning of the 19th June.

I have hurried over our march as it afforded nothing worthy of note. We never saw the face of a French soldier since the evening of the 18th, nor did any individual of the British army till arriving near the fortified heights of Montmartre, near Paris, which capitulated the next day. On the 4th, the remnant of the French army filed off to Orleans where they now are.

Yours, etc. etc.

CHAPTER EIGHT

Napoleon's Apologia Pro Vita Sua given on board HMS Northumberland 6 August 1815

After much deliberation and heart searching combined with pushing from the National Assembly, Napoleon decided to surrender to the British in the shape of HMS Bellerophon, *(Captain Maitland RN), which was guarding the port of Rochefort.*
Captain Maitland accepted the surrender, provided that his illustrious prisoner was prepared to place himself at the disposition of the British Government.

In a fulsome letter to the Prince Regent which remained unanswered Bonaparte did what was required of him.
Not until the end of July however was the decision made by the Allies in concert that St. Helena was to be his destination.
On 7th August, Bonaparte was transferred to HMS Northumberland *having been informed of his fate the day before by Lord Keith and Sir George Cockburn.*

Admiral Sir George Cockburn (1772-1853) who was addressed as "General" by Napoleon when he came aboard Northumberland, *had already had a distinguished career in the Navy which he had joined at the age of nine. He eventually became (in 1851) an Admiral of the Fleet. He was now to be Bonaparte's temporary jailer on St Helena pending the arrival of Sir Hudson Lowe*(1).

Bonaparte succeeded in charming everyone with whom he came into contact on board Northumberland, *even Lord Keith. It is probably as well, therefore, that he was kept at arms' length from many on shore in England, including the Prince Regent.*

The unknown writer of the following narrative has obviously taken it down verbatim, often in note form. It is most probably Cockburn himself. Whoever it was had a rare opportunity to judge the character of the prisoner.

Hardly an apologia, it is more a tissue of excuses, prevarications and evasions for and of the various crimes of which he had been accused. The reader himself must be the final judge after satisfying himself regarding the time facts of the various cases cited.

Was the prisoner's lapse in calling Cockburn "General" due to his notorious ignorance of sea power or to an inherent dislike of all things naval, as a result of the many disasters suffered by his own fleet?

6th August, 1815.

Sir George Cockburn and Lord Keith went on board [HMS] *Bellerophon* and informed Bonaparte that he was to remove the next day into [HMS] *Northumberland* and proceed on to St. Helena. Bonaparte protested against the right of the British Government to dispose of him. Sir George Cockburn did not enter into the merits of the question but observed that as military officers they must obey the instructions of their government and hoped Bonaparte would be ready the next morning to go on board [HMS] *Northumberland.*

August 7th. Sir George Cockburn went on board to examine the baggage of Bonaparte, etc., and all arms were delivered to him. Sir George Cockburn took 4,000 Napoleons(2) in gold which he sent to the Treasury by Captain Maitland.

Bonaparte was with the Grand Marshal Compte de Bertrand, Madame Bertrand, their three children, the Grand Compte le Montholon, Madame Montholon and one child, Le Compte de las Casas, his son thirteen years old, General Gourgaud, seven grown up persons, one young gentleman, five children, two women and twelve men servants; in all twenty-seven persons.

When he was on deck Bonaparte said, "Here I am, General, (sic) at your orders", addressing himself to Sir George Cockburn. He then asked to be introduced to the Captain and officers with whom he conversed. He ate very heartily at dinner and almost of every dish, praised everything at dinner and seemed reconciled and contented with his fate.

He talked much of his Russian campaign: said he meant only to refresh his troops at Moscow for four or five days and then to have marched towards Petersburg, but the destruction of Moscow disconcerted all his projects. He spoke of villages in flames done by the natives and as of marching through a sea of fire! Of the cold on his return: one night half of his guard were frozen to death. After coffee he walked on deck: played at Vingt-et-un and went to bed between ten and eleven. He seemed quite at home and at his ease - very seasick the next and following day.

General Gourgaud told Sir George Cockburn that Grouchy had between 30 and 40,000 (men) and that Bonaparte was forced off the field by Soult.

Bertrand said that Bonaparte landed with only 600 men from Elba and that he had no communication with any of the Marshals: adopted the plan from his own idea on reading in the papers how unwisely the Bourbons were acting and knowing therefore they would be unpopular throughout France and he had only to show himself to ensure his being joined by everybody.

That he had determined on the invasion of England when his army was at Boulogne: disappointed by his fleet not obeying his orders to proceed to the Channel:

then the plan was given up: meant to have got as near Chatham as possible and then pushed for London: determined afterwards to proceed against Austria: attacked Mack (Goldsmith's Secret History Correct).

When Bonaparte was within five leagues of Grenoble a detachment of the 5th Regiment was disposed to oppose him. He put himself immediately in front and throwing open his great coat to show himself more conspicuously called to them to kill their Emperor if they wished it. This had the desired effect he expected and they all joined him and afterwards he received nothing but congratulations on his way to Paris.

He said he had paid too much attention to the Jacobin Party and had better have depended on his own popularity.

The conduct of the Allies forced him to form his army and move with it so quickly. He had no time to examine it and weed it as he should have done and therefore many officers remained in it who had received their appointment from the Bourbons and were disaffected to him: he did not lose any soldiers by desertion but the officers were constantly deserting on the march. He paid a compliment to the lower orders of people in France at the expense of the higher orders. He said that the former were the most sincere, the most firm, and at the same time the best dispositioned people in the world, but as you rose in the classes of people in France the characters became worse and above all the bourgeois. They were too fickle and volatile to be at all depended upon. They had one principle for today and another for tomorrow according to the circumstances of the moment and he attributed solely to the officers of the army his Waterloo disaster.

He told Sir George Cockburn he knew early in the day the Prussians were on his flank: that this gave little or no uneasiness as he depended on Grouchy also closing with him at the same time and he had ordered a sufficient force to oppose these Prussians who were in fact already checked: that he considered the battle on the whole rather in his favour than otherwise throughout the day but after dusk the disaffected officers he had alluded to spread the cry of "sauve qui peut" which caused such confusion and alarm through the whole line that it became impossible to counteract it or to rally his troops: that treachery and darkness combined rendered his ruin inevitable.

He said that on the morning of 18th June he did not entertain the remotest idea that the Duke of Wellington would have allowed him to have brought the English army to a decisive battle and he therefore had been the more anxious to push on and if possible to force it as he considered nothing else could offer a chance of surmounting the difficulties with which he was surrounded, but he added if he could have beaten the English army, which from the approximation of their respective numbers he was led to consider, the situation was such that he was positive hardly any of the English forces would have escaped being either taken or killed. The Prussian army, having already been beaten on the 16th, (upon any decisive disaster of the English) would have been forced to make a precipitate retreat and perhaps have been dispersed, certainly disorganised. He then might have pushed by forced marches to have met the Austrians before any junction could have taken place between them and the Russians, which would have placed the game in his hands if hostilities had been obstinately perservered in, though in the latter stage of things he had built, he said, rather on the idea that victory over the English army in Belgium with its immediate results would have been sufficient to produce a change of Administration in England and might have afforded him a chance of concluding an immediate general truce. [That] was really his first object as France was hardly equal to the effort she was then making and it was perfectly impossible for him to think of making an adequate resistance against the numerous forces of the Allies if once united and acting in concert against him.

Alexander advised Bonaparte to set aside Josephine. At first he did not wish it. Alexander proposed he should marry a Russian princess: difficulties and impediments however were thrown in the way though Josephine had assented to the arrangement. Eugene Beauharnais his son-in-law (step son) pressed upon him an alliance with an Austrian princess. Bonaparte consented if it could be done at once.

He said that after the Emperor of Austria's behaviour he could not bring himself to apply to Austria for protection. He thought that the English had used him ill but [was] still glad he was under the protection of English laws: under any other his fate might have depended on the will of an individual.

Bonaparte observed to Sir George Cockburn that he had been placed in chief command at 24 years of age as a general officer, that he had made the conquest of Italy at twenty-five; that he had risen from nothing to be a sovereign of his country as Consul at thirty and that if chance had caused him to have died or have been killed the day after he entered Moscow that his would have been a career of advancement and uninterrupted success without a parallel. The very misfortunes which afterwards befell the French army would in such a case probably rather have tended to the advantage than to the disadvantage of his fame, as however inevitable they were they would certainly then have been rather attributed to his loss than the true cause.

He considered the Russians and Poles to be decidely a braver race of people than all the rest of Europe excepting the French and English.

He said the Emperor of Austria had neither abilities nor firmness of character: that the King of Prussia was "un pauvre bête": that Alexander was a more active and clever man than any of the other sovereigns of Europe but that he was extremely false; that Russia was much to be feared if Poland was not preserved as an independent nation [and] that after his arrival at Paris from Elba, he had received assurances from both the King of Spain and from the Portuguese that whatever appearances they might be forced to make, he might depend upon their taking no action or offensive pact against him.

He professed to entertain a high respect for the late Lord Cornwallis and of Fox but not of many other characters in England. He had gained possession of a correspondence from a foreign Royal personage of great consideration (Duc d'Orleans probably) who spoke disrespectfully of different branches of our Royal Family. He observed the nations of the continent were not adapted to a representative government; that he had submitted to popular feelings, not that he considered it a wise measure for the French.

When his army in Egypt was so severely visited by the plague the soldiers and indeed the officers became so disheartened that he found it necessary in order to give them confidence to visit the hospitals himself and talk to and cheer up the patients and that he caught the disorder but got rid of it directly. Those who kept up their spirits generally revived, those who despaired generally died. The Jaffa poisoning story - He said that finding himself obliged to evacuate Jaffa and leave it to the possession of Djezzar Pasha[(3)] whose cruelty of character was well known he ordered off before him all the sick and wounded of the army who could be moved. To facilitate which he lent even his own horses. But the chief physician then represented that there were a few Frenchmen in such an advanced stage of the plague that there did [not] remain even a possibility of their recovery and that attempting to move them with the rest would endanger the whole army. Knowing however as he (B) well did if these unhappy creatures fell into the hands of Djezzar Pasha all sorts of cruelties would be practised on them in their last moments, he felt the best thing he could do was to order a council of all the medical men of the army to assemble to ascertain in the first place whether the removal of these people might be effected without endangering in an unwarrantable degree the rest of the army, and whether there existed any chance of adequate benefit accruing to themselves if their removal was attempted. In the next place if the council agreed with the chief physician and confirmed the absolute necessity of some being let behind, then to consider if it would not be better for the individuals themselves to accelerate their death by opium rather than to leave them in the state they then were, to be tormented by the implacable enemies into whose hands they were inevitably to fall. He said the council was public and everybody knew what passed in it.

The medical council reported it their decided and unanimous opinion that these people ought not on any account to be removed yet. The majority could not bear the idea of adopting such a measure, accelerating the death of individuals under their care however desperate their condition, but they further stated that they had every reason to believe all difficulties on this head would be done away by the natural process of the disease if he (B) could retain the place 48 hours longer.

Upon this report he (B) determined in keeping Jaffa the time specified and he continued in it himself with the whole army twenty-four hours then left a strong rear-guard to hold it the other twenty-four hours at which time he said the predictions of the medical officers were nearly confirmed by the death of almost everyone of the patients in question, though perhaps one or two had been left not quite dead. He considered the measure which he wished to have adopted as more deserving of praise than censure. If he had been one of the people afflicted he should have thought it the greatest act of kindness to have been so dealt with rather than to be left without hope of recovery to be tortured by such cruel savages as the Pasha's troops. (This part of the statement was afterwards confirmed to Sir George Cockburn by Captain Beattie of the Marines, who belonged to the Theseus off Egypt who entered Jaffa immediately after the French had quitted and even before the troops of the Pasha. He said there were only three or four Frenchmen found alive in it and those in an advanced state of the disease.

At Tilsit[4] he [was] baffled at the Queen of Prussia's personal requests that the town of Magdeberg might by that treaty be left to Prussia. The Queen sadly chagrined. Bonaparte said he thought her a most elegant, engaging woman and as handsome as a woman of thirty-five could be. He spoke very ill of her character as a wife and particularly with reference to the Emperor Alexander to oblige whom he mentioned, (as a joke), that he detained the King of Prussia[5] a whole day by announcing an intention of paying him a formal visit, of which Alexander took premeditated advantage by setting to get thereby an uninterrupted tête-a-tête visit with the Queen!

Bonaparte assured Sir George Cockburn that had he been successful in the Russian campaign all he should have asked would have been the independence of Poland, (but he probably had more extensive views, for at Moscow he dispersed emissaries among the Russian peasantry to bias them in his favour and against their own government).

Previous to the death of Paul[6] he had received seven or eight letters from Paul himself to add their united strength to humble Great Britain and Paul proposed to send off at once a large Russian army to act against the English in India.

Bonaparte had corresponded and had communication with the disaffected Protestants in Ireland as well as Catholics.

A few years ago Bonaparte caused a survey of the grown oaks in France to be made and [found] that there was actually sufficient to build a thousand ships of the line, but that France failed altogether in trees for masts.

Bonaparte said he had in the field at the Battle of Wagram under his command more men than in any of his other battles: they amounted to 180,000 and 1,000 pieces of cannon. At Moscow he had not quite so many but not far short: at Leipsich not more than 140,000. He said that General Clausel was decidedly the most able military officer now in France. Soult and the other Marshals brave men for carrying into execution operations previously planned, but to plan and execute with large armies none were equal to Clausel.

Bonaparte told Sir George Cockburn that it was owing to the want of officers at the beginning of the Revolutionary War which caused him to be sent for, (though then a very young captain of artillery), from the northern frontier where he was serving, to take command of the artillery of the army before Toulon. Almost immediately after his arrival he pointed out to General Carteaux the necessity of taking possession of the place called by the English, Mulgrave. General Carteaux would not listen to him: the attack went on as usual when on one of the representatives of the people coming to overlook what they were about, (which was customary in those times), Bonaparte laid before him his plans. They were approved of and General Carteaux directed to adopt what Bonaparte had suggested which succeeded completely. In reward he was immediately promoted in rank to General of Brigade. He afterwards went into Savoy but it falling to his lot to be drafted into the infantry with some other artillery officers in consequence of want of infantry officers, he quitted the army and went to Paris to remonstrate and endeavour to prevent the Exchange but, meeting with an unfavourable reception from a general of artillery who was a representative of the people with whom he had high words, Bonaparte retired in disgust and putting on the dress of the Institute of Paris to which he belonged, (having been elected for his proficiency in mathematics), he remained quiet in Paris.

On the advance of the Austrians under De Vins into Italy and the retreat of the French army opposed to him, which spread great consternation in Paris, the Committee of Public Safety knowing that he (B) was acquainted with the locality of that country sent for him to consult on the best measures to be adopted and they were so well satisfied with his suggestions that they made him draw up instructions for their General in Italy and kept him near them in Paris to assist in further military points. The advice he gave proved efficacious: the Italian army took up [the] positions he marked out and maintained them against the efforts of the Austrians; was reinforced and then attacked and in its turn defeated De Vins. Bonaparte gained great credit on this account. He remained at Paris till the 13 Vendemiaire(7), the day on which the Convention was attacked by the revolted Sections of Paris who obtained very great advantage over the troops of the Convention.

The Committee of Public Safety sent for Bonaparte and placed him at the head of their troops. He defeated those of the Sections and restored order. In reward for this he was made Commandant of Paris which gave him much consequence. He remained there until he was appointed Commander-in-Chief of the Army of Italy but he told Sir George Cockburn that it was not until the Battle of Lodi(8) that any idea of his becoming of sufficient consequence to authority at a future day [or thought of] interference in the government of France entered his mind when, finding all his plans succeeded beyond his own expectations, he began to look forward though without decided plans. That the quantity of money he sent into France from Italy with these views increased his popularity but after his campaign in Italy, and the suspension of hostilities with Austria which followed, the Directory grew very jealous of him and were very anxious to get him into a scrape.

To avoid it required all his caution and finesse and induced him to refuse the appointment offered him to conduct diplomatic discussions then going on with Austria, as also the other appointment soon afterwards offered to him to command an army for the invasion of England. When the command of an expedition to Egypt was proposed he saw directly the advantages it opened of getting out of the way of a jealous arbitrary government.

After leaving France he was ever anxiously looking for those events which brought him back even before they happened and his return being well assured there was no party strong enough to oppose him. He planned immediately the revolution of 18 Brumaire(9) for on that day the government of France fell into his hands and those of his adherents.

The attempt of Pichegru, Georges (Cadoudal) and, he added, Moreau(10) was the nearest of any proving fatal to him. Thirty-six of the party had actually been in Paris six weeks without the police knowing anything of them. When it was at last discovered by means of an emigrant apothecary who had been informed against and secured for landing from an English man-of-war, the police, entertaining suspicions from the numbers reported to have clandestinely landed about the same time, judged the apothecary would be a likely person to bring to a confession if well managed. Therefore being condemned to die and every preparation made for the execution, his life was then offered if he would make any disclosure sufficiently important to deserve a pardon. He instantly caught at the offer and gave the names of thirty-six persons everyone of whom, with Pichegru and Georges (Cadoudal), were found and secured in Paris within a fortnight. He (B) said that previously to this plot being discovered it would probably have proved fatal to him had not Georges (Cadoudal) insisted on being appointed a Consul which Moreau and Pichegru would not hear of and therefore Georges (Cadoudal) and his party could not be brought to act. He said it was to be at hand ready to aid in these conspiracies and take advantage of them that the Duc d'Enghien[11] went to reside in the neighbourhood of Strasbourg in which town he (B) had certain intelligence of the Duc having been in disguise several times. He added that the Duc was condemned for having conspired against France and he was determined from the first to let the law take its course: to endeavour if possible to check the repeated conspiracies.

In answer to Sir George Cockburn remonstrating against his having taken the Duc from the territory of the Duke of Baden he said that this did not in his opinion at all alter the case as between France and the Duc d'Enghien: that the Duke of Baden might indeed have some reason to complain of the violation of his territory but that was an affair for him to settle with the Duke of Baden and not with the Duc d'Enghien, who when they had got within French territory (no matter how), they had full right to try and punish for any act against the existing government committed by him in France.

On Bonaparte's arrival at St. Helena he complained of the crowd that gathered in the town to see him and at his own request resided at the Briars, a small house at a short distance.

Speaking of Captain Wright, Bonaparte said that when Lord Ebrington at Elba first drew his attention to the name and circumstances of the case he did not recollect them which he said was exactly this: that Captain Wright being supposed in France to have been concerned in the conspiracy of George (Cadoudal) and the others was, when taken, conveyed to the Temple[12] preparatory to examination and on being ordered to attend a council charged with the investigation of it, put an end to himself. Bonaparte, though he confessed he could give no reason for Captain Wright committing such an act, added that the inferior rank and little consequence of that officer ought to have exempted him from the charge of having either ordered or attached importance to his death.

Baron de Kolly was first found out by his endeavouring to gain over some person to his interests in Paris, as also from a suspicion excited by the command of money which he seemed to possess, that upon his being arrested all his papers were discovered and then it was determined to send off a police officer to Paris to personate Kolly at Valensay to deliver the Prince Regent's letter and to assure Ferdinand[20] that everything was prepared for his escape, purposely to prove how he would act under such circumstances: but in spite of everything their sham Kolly could urge, (Bonaparte added he was a clever fellow), Ferdinand's courage was not equal to the undertaking and he obstinately refused to have anything to do with the pretended Kolly.

In a letter from Paris in July 1815 by W D Fellows the author mentions that he had the last autumn become acquainted with an officer who had served with Captain Wright when taken. This officer said he had just escaped from a long imprisonment in France during which he had been three years in Solitary confinement in the dungeons of the Temple and other prisons and was afterwards removed to Verdun from whence he had escaped by jumping from the ramparts into the Meuse.

After enduring painful fatigues and privations and evading the police by impersonating a Polish Jew he reached the sea coast (of Flanders) and was taken aboard an English frigate by some fishermen whom he had bribed with the money he had provided himself with.

A guide who left Verdun with him treacherously deserted him after stealing his valise (supposing it contained his money) while he lay asleep in a wood. The cash had been, however, secreted round his body.

This officer said Captain Wright was murdered after being put to the torture twice. A short time before he perished Captain Wright wrote to him desiring that if he survived he would make known that he had been tortured. This officer had himself been repeatedly threatened with the torture. Captain Wright was attended by a French surgeon employed in the Temple: through him Captain Wright communicated to his friend the details of his sufferings.

---

(1) General Sir Hudson Lowe (1769-1844) was Governor of St Helena during Napoleon's period of exile.

(2) A Napoleon was a gold coin bearing a portrait of Napoleon.

(3) Ahmed Djezzar Pasha (1735-1804) was nicknamed 'The Butcher'. As Governor of Acre in the Lebanon, he successfully defended the town against Napoleon during the siege of 1799 (18 March - 20 May) when he had the backing of Sidney Smith and a Royal Navy flotilla.

(4) The Peace and Treaties of Tilsit, 7 and 9 July 1807. Following the battle of Friedland, Napoleon and Alexander 1 of Russia met in June 1807 for private peace discussions. At Tilsit, Alexander abandoned his former ally, Frederick III of Prussia for a 'reversal of alliances' and on 7 July a peace treaty, secret articles and an agreement of alliance were signed. Two days later, a separate treaty dealt with Prussia in a severely punitive fashion.

(5) King Frederick William III of Prussia (1770-1840) succeeded to the throne in 1797. He left the Third Coalition in 1805 after Austerlitz but encouraged by his patriotic and Francophobe wife Queen Louise (described by Napoleon as 'the only real man in Prussia') he formed a Fourth Coalition and issued an ultimatum to Napoleon. Defeats at Jena and Auerstadt ruined Prussia militarily and later in the Treaties of Tilsit - and in spite of Queen Louise appealing in person to Napoleon for favourable terms - Prussia was broken up and Prussian soldiers ordered to fight for the French. A huge war indemnity had to be paid and Frederick became no more than a French puppet ruler. In 1813 he threw over the French

alliance, joined the Sixth Coalition and subsequently his troops fought in every campaign against the French up to Waterloo.

(6) Tsar Paul 1 of Russia (1754-1801) was assassinated in 1801 and was succeeded by his son Alexander 1.

(7) Vendemaire - the month of the grape harvest was the first month of the French revolutionary calendar and ran from 23 September to 22 October.

(8) The Battle of Lodi on 10 May 1796 was a violent confrontation during the second phase of the 1796 campaign in Italy which helped to strengthen Napoleon's ascendency. His personal supervision of the siting of the French guns led to his being nicknamed 'le petit caporal' because it was normally the duty of an artillery corporal to align the cannons.

(9) Brumaire - the month of mist (from the french word *brume* – mist) was the second month of the French revolutionary calender and lasted from 23 October - 21 November. The 18th Brumaire (9 November 1799) was the day on which the Directory fell and Napoleon established his supremacy.

(10) General Jean Charles Pichegru (1761-1804) had held a number of senior military commands before resigning as commander of the Army of the Rhine and Moselle when the Austrians took Mainz. He became President of the Council of Five Hundred but was condemned after the coup d'etat of 1797 and was deported to Guiana, from where he escaped to London.

Georges Cadoudal (1771-1804) was a royalist conspirator. He helped to mastermind an attempt on Napoleon's life in 1800. After escaping to England he returned to plot with Pichegru and Moreau, a former Army commander, in the conspiracy which bears his name which ended in an abortive attempt to ambush Napoleon in January 1804. Cadoudal was arrested and executed in June 1804. Napoleon's Minister of Police, Fouché used the conspiracy as an excuse to eliminate many political enemies.

(11) Louis, Duc d'Enghien (1772-1804) was son of an ancient French family with royal connections. Because of the number of royalist plots, Napoleon ordered Enghien's (illegal) arrest on neutral territory in March 1804. He was tried in a military court with no defence and shot. The act shocked Europe and was a factor in the formation of the Third Coalition against France.

(12) The Temple in Paris was originally the stronghold of the Knights Templar and was later the home of the Knights of St John. The old tower then became a prison where, in 1792 the French royal family was incarcerated. From there, Louis XVI, Marie Antoinette and Princess Elizabeth were taken to the guillotine while the Dauphin probably died within the prison walls. It was demolished by Napoleon in the early years of the Empire.

Napoleon

CHAPTER NINE

Artillery at Waterloo from Paris – 25 August 1815

The following letter gives an account of the artillery at Waterloo. The "Sir" is presumed to be Allan but the signatory A J Frason remains a mystery.

At first it was thought that it could be another fault of transcription and might be Frazer. Sir Augustus Frazer was a well-known Gunner Officer and commanded the Horse Artillery at Waterloo. Frazer's second initial is, however, "S" and it is hardly possible that there could be two consecutive faults.

There is no A J Frason in the Waterloo Roll Call, the list of RA officers, or the Army List and no Fraser or Frazer answers to this description. It is interesting to note that no mention is made of rockets except as fougasses. These were one of Wellington's pet aversions since they were apt to backfire and cause more damage to ones' own side than to the enemy.

Artillery Waterloo
25 August 1815
Hotel du Nord, Rue de Richelieu.

My dear Sir,

I find on referring to some memoranda relating to Waterloo that at the beginning of the affair there were in the first line fifty-four pieces of artillery from the road leading to Nivelle to that leading towards La Belle Alliance – and thirty from that road to the extreme left of the position.

The Artillery at first were thus placed – first line – one troop of Horse Artillery to keep in check troops advancing by the road leading from Nivelle. One troop of howitzers brought up to drive the enemy out of the wood and orchard of the Chateau of Hougoumont another troop and eight fougasses (rockets?) formed to play on the masses of the enemy forming to their left of La Belle Alliance - Two troops of Horse Artillery and one brigade of foot Artillery (being the reserve artillery) placed to the right of La Haye Sainte, these guns obliquely on the road leading to La Belle Alliance (to fire) at the troops forming to the enemy's left of it. To the immediate left of the road by La Haye Sainte was a troop of Horse Artillery, to its left were three brigades of Artillery - to the extreme left of all was a troop of Horse Artillery. These last mentioned troops and brigades played on the troops in their direct front and were considered in some measure as more disposable (*sic*) than those to the right of the road leading to La Belle Alliance.

In the second line the guns were thus placed. Two troops of Horse Artillery formed on the right of the second line in the manner called "in potence" or thus

line
line
g
u
n
s

for the purpose of repelling any attack made between Braine l'Allend and the Nivelle road. A brigade of Foot Artillery with part of its guns guarding a hollow road to the right. Another brigade and a troop of Horse Artillery formed near the centre of the second line.

Towards the close of the day the troops guarding the Nivelle Road on the right of the first line, after having been beaten from its position, had recovered it.

Eight troops of Horse Artillery and five brigades of Foot Artillery remained posted between the immediate front of the Chateau of Hougoumont and La Haye Sainte. The guns had frequently lost the crest of the hill and both from recoiling without having been again run up and from an endeavour to bring up as many as possible, were found much closer than usual. Several were run out of the line and were forced to their left just towards the conclusion and just before the last desperate attack of which I was aware, being informed of it by a Colonel of French Cuirassiers who came over with the information.

In the valley between the first line and the position previously occupied by the second were disabled guns, carriages and ammunition waggons, of which some had been blown up during the day. Near La Haye Sainte the guns were much disabled.

Three brigades and one troop remained in their position to the left of the road.

The enemy's guns were frequently formed in two lines of which the rear fired over the heads of the front one. Besides the guns formed as it were in battery in our immediate front, guns to the right of the Nivelles road took our line obliquely and others formed to the left of the road leading to La Haye Sainte did the same. None of the enemy's guns were dismounted in the fields, the British artillery having strict orders to fire on the troops disregarding the enemy's guns.

The sky was particularly lucid towards the conclusion of the day and there was no dust.

In the repeated charges of the enemy's brave cavalry the guns were abandoned by order, the gunners sheltering themselves by the sides of the square of infantry, then resuming their post at the guns. Generally speaking these squares did not fire. Relative to the Horse Artillery, now armed with heavier guns than usual, it may be well to remark that the guns had ten Horse Artillery men mounted with each and that eight draft horses were attached to each gun. All the howitzers engaged were heavy, the same as at Vitoria.

Yours etc.
A J FRASON

British Artillery

CHAPTER 10

A Letter from Ben Sydenham to Allan from Paris – 5 November 1815

This letter from Ben Sydenham to Allan as late as November 1815 gives, as the result of a personal interview, the Duke of Wellington's own estimate of the numbers engaged on both sides at Waterloo.

These figures should be compared with those given by Lord Fitzroy Somerset in Chapter 6.

Paris, Hotel de la Paix
5 Nov. 1815

My dear Allan,

Your letter reached me very opportunely for soon after I got it Lord Wellington came to take leave of me, and gave me an opportunity of speaking to him on the subject of your enquiry.

I start for Nice early tomorrow. Lord W began by reminding me of the extreme difficulty of procuring any accurate accounts of [the] enemy's or even of your own forces on a day of battle. I can answer for the truth of this, for when I was in Spain, although he furnished me with daily intelligence returns and what would be considered ample materials, I was neither able to satisfy either him or myself concerning the comparative strengths of the French and allied armies. We often succeeded in approaching to the truth, but were sometimes grossly deceived in our calculations. Lord Wellington heard of no intercepted returns from which could be determined the strength of thc army with which Bonaparte invaded Flanders or the amount of their losses or their actual force at the Battle of Waterloo. From all Lord Wellington heard in Flanders and since his arrival in Paris, he is disposed to estimate the extreme force of the French army in crossing the Sambre at 130,000 men of all arms. He thinks that they lost at the Battle of Ligny and previous affairs 20,000 men (I believe this is beyond the truth), hors de combat and Ney has publicly declared that he lost 5,000 against the English and Belgians at Quatre Bras etc. They therefore had 105,000 men on the morning of the 18th. The two corps under Grouchy amounted in round numbers to 20,000 so that they brought 85,000 against Lord Wellingtons position in front of Mont St Jean. This is all the information Lord Wellington possesses on the subject and it appears to me useless to seek further intelligence.

Clarke, the Minister of War, told Lord W that Bonaparte had 89,000 under his *immediate* command on the 18th June – Lord W can, of course, tell you pretty nearly the amount of the British forces in action, but his information of the various Gothic and Celtic tribes of which his miscellaneous army was composed is less accurate, but he thinks he had in all about 84,000 men of all nations on the 15th. He lost 5,000 men at Quatre Bras which leaves him 79,000. Of this number Prince Frederick of Orange was detached to Halle with:-

12,000	Belgians
4,000	British
1,300	Estoff's legion
450	2nd German Hussars
17,750	

which leaves 61,250 to occupy the position of Mont St Jean and this Lord W considers to be a fair estimate of his actual strength on the 18th June in round numbers: this gives Bonaparte one fourth more than Lord Wellington.

etc. etc. etc, B.S.

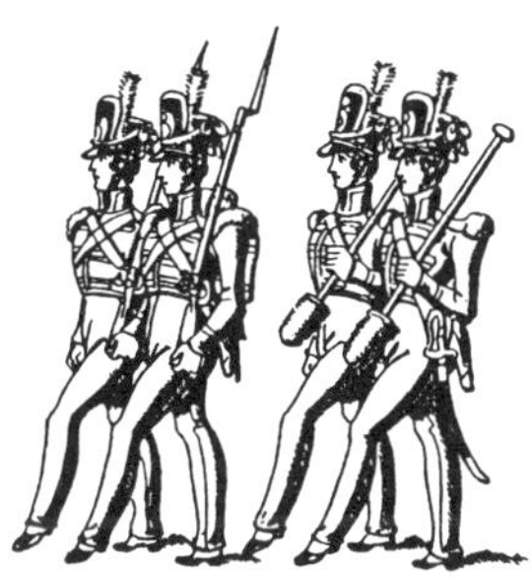

British Artillery

CHAPTER 11

Two letters from the Marquess of Anglesey to Allan – 9 and 18 December 1815

The two following letters to Allan are from the Marquess of Anglesey who as the Earl of Uxbridge commanded the cavalry at Waterloo.

Henry William Paget, who became the first Marquess of Anglesey, had eloped with Lady Charlotte Wellesley, wife of Wellington's brother Henry. This elopement and the subsequent divorce had caused great scandal in London.

It is probable that the Duke would have preferred Stapleton Cotton (Lord Combermere) who had commanded the cavalry in Spain. The cause of this preference was not the divorce, however, but because the two men had never served together.

To someone who suggested to the Duke that Lord Uxbridge had the reputation of running away with everyone he could, Wellington replied "I'll take good care he don't run away with me. I don't care about anybody else".

Uxbridge had a brilliant reputation which was justified by his handling of the cavalry during the retirement from Quatre Bras. Wellington was always critical of the cavalry and their precipitate charges. At Waterloo this of course happened with Uxbridge in the first line so consequently these charges were unstoppable until too late and heavy losses were suffered.

Late in the action Uxbridge lost his leg. "By God! I've lost my leg!" "Have you, by God?" was a somewhat typical reply by the preoccupied Duke. War has little time for sentiment.

Copy of a letter from the Marquess of Anglesey to Colonel Allan.

Beaudessert 9 Dec 1815

My dear Sir

Lady Anglesey has just found the sketch of the quarters of the Cavalry and

Horse Artillery which I now forward to you with another cover, and she begs you to return it as soon as you have done with it.

In compliance with your wishes I add what were our movements before the 18th June. All the Cavalry and Horse Artillery moved from their cantonments between 5 and 6 o'clock a.m. on the 16th by brigades and made a forced march to Quatre Bras which they reached that night. The Light Dragoons only arrived before the close of the action but they were not engaged.

At day break of the 17th the enemy occupied the ground he had taken up the evening before.

No certain intelligence arrived on the result of the battle between the Prussians and the French until towards 6 o'clock when it was ascertained that Blücher's centre had been forced and he had been compelled to retire upon Wavre. This determined the Duke of Wellington to fall back and I was ordered with the whole of the Cavalry and Horse Artillery and with some battalions of Light Infantry to cover the retreat of the Army which was in motion by 10 o'clock.

All was quiet until 1 p.m. when a very large body of the enemy's cavalry and artillery showed themselves upon the high ground of the left of Quatre Bras and which had come from the pursuit of the Prussians.

After a short pause it advanced and the necessary dispositions being by that time made and the light battalions withdrawn, the Cavalry began its retreat in three columns over the river to Genappe.

The centre column consisting of all the Heavy Cavalry, the Horse Artillery and two regiments of Hussars and Light Dragoons passed the river by folds. Some skirmishing and a trifling cannonade took place in front of the river, but the whole crossed without any serious affair. Nothing followed the flank columns beyond the river: but the rearguard of the centre column was closely pressed through Genappe and on the other side when they formed, became so troublesome that it was necessary to check their impetuosity; for this purpose our Hussars were ordered to attack their advance-guard consisting of Lancers, and a very spirited attack being soon after made by the Life Guards it had the desired effect.

The enemy now brought up cannon and deployed. They attempted to move up on our right but this effort was effectually foiled by the well executed movements of Sir W. Ponsonby's Brigade and the heavy state of the ground making it by this time obvious that the enemy could not gain our flank the whole was drawn in upon the main road and then retired slowly into the position of Waterloo.

There was a great deal of skirmishing and cannonading during the retreat which was effected in perfect order.

The Duke of Wellington prepared a battery in his position which opened fire as the cavalry entered it. He stopped the enemy's advance and thus finished the affair.

The cavalry bivouacked for the night in the second line. You know all about the battle of the 18th so I remain,

Yours very faithfully,
Anglesey.

2nd letter from Lord Anglesey.

Beaudessert 18th Dec 1815

My dear Sir,

I am very glad the slight sketch I gave you of the movements of the cavalry up to the 18th June and the plan of their quarters were acceptable to you.

I wish I could furnish you with what you want for the 18th but I feel if I undertook it as if I should be writing a history of my own exploits. I will however just mark the outline of the cavalry operations.

The manouevres were very few; it was almost all straight forward fighting. I kept them [my men] chiefly in the second line to the infantry and fell upon the French cavalry whenever it attempted to penetrate.

The most destructive attack was made perhaps about two o'clock upon two very large masses of infantry and cavalry who tried to force our centre.

I ordered Sir W Ponsonby, (a most gallant officer and excellent fellow), to fall upon them with his brigade. Almost at the same moment I took down Lord Edward Somerset with the Household Brigade for the same purpose. Both succeeded. They overthrew everything before them: two Eagles and above 2,500 prisoners were taken in these charges: they bore down the cavalry and penetrated the squares of infantry and really destroyed an immense number of men. They pressed too far and suffered severely principally from the enemy's artillery.

Sir W Ponsonby's brigade was very much exposed and constantly engaged during the day, charged very often, and always with success.

Sir C Grant was upon the right. His brigade was also very much exposed during the whole day and frequently and most gallantly repelled the enemy's attack. It was this brigade I sent to get upon the enemy's left flank when they had three regiments of Lancers and some guns which flanked and greatly annoyed our right.

The movement was very judiciously made and Grant was about to follow on when he perceived a very heavy attack made upon our centre. Fearing then, in the event of its success, which was more probable from the immense force of Cuirassiers which was leading it and knowing how few cavalry we had then, he, having forced the enemy to withdraw, immediately returned within our position.

Colonel Arenschilde's brigade was also occasionally engaged and in the evening Sir C Vandeleur(2) (sic) and Sir R Vivian's (sic) were brought from the left and arrived at the critical moment when the enemy were giving way in all directions. They attacked with great vigour and did them much mischief.

Sir C Grant's and Baron Dornberg joined in the pursuit.

The Dutch and Belgian cavalry and Brunswickers were in line and suffered a great deal. All the Horse Artillery were in position, did great execution and suffered much.

This is a short and very imperfect sketch of the movements of the Cavalry and Horse Artillery and I beg you to consider it *totally, solely, for your private eye*. If you want more interesting details and individual exploits I know nobody to whom you had better apply than to my Aide-de-Camp Captain Wildman of the 7th who has heard all the stories and will not object to telling them.

As for the infantry I say nothing as you have much better sources of information, but this I must say, that no coolness, gallantry or steadiness ever equalled theirs, their several chiefs and our great chiefs. I dwell at this moment with wonder at all I witnessed in them.

I remain ever truly yours.

Anglesey

Sir John Ormsby Vandeleur

Sir Hussey Vivian

---

(1) Sir Colquhoun Grant (1764-1835) commanded a Hussar brigade at Waterloo. He was promoted Lieutenant General in 1830.

(2) Sir John Ormsby Vandeleur (1763-1849) commanded the 4th Cavalry Brigade at Waterloo. He was promoted General in 1838.

Life Guards

INTRODUCTION TO THE APPENDICES

by Edward Owen

Comparisons of character are not only odious but also difficult, even when those compared are poles apart. The old saying that it is better to be respected than popular is probably true in the long run. The word love is not really suitable in this context since it has so many shades of meaning, from a no-score in tennis to a deep abiding passion.

For respect, perhaps integrity is a better word and in this case popular may be considered to be a popularity bordering on idolatory.
If Wellington represents integrity then Napoleon represents such popularity. How then is the equation to be solved? The answer is that in the short term both equal nought.

Wellington carried his integrity into politics in which field of human endeavour the word is a dirty one. The Duke consequently lost the battle in the morass of the Reform Bill, but won the final victory in that he regained the respect and even veneration of all until his death.

Popularity feeds on success. When failure begins to show such feelings begin to wane. Peter Arno in one of his New Yorker cartoons makes the "Lady" say to the erstwhile millionaire "When you sold your yacht something in me died". Napoleon received enormous adulation from the French – and an equally fierce rejection by them. The "Roses, Roses, all the way . . ." syndrome is too familiar, especially among politically volatile peoples. How quickly are the "laurel and the rose" snatched away.

Napoleon too returned to favour; his tomb in the Invalides is a national shrine.

Both these men came through great tribulation to final acclaim by their respective nations.

Wellington overrode the storm in his lifetime, Napoleon did so only by his death and by the courtesy of his former enemies.

It is ironic that the British probably take more interest in Napoleon than do the French if the number of books about him are taken into account.

This phenomenon is probably the result of that typically English sentiment; he played very well, I only just managed to beat him.

The tombs in St. Paul's and the Invalides are the only true symbols of the fall of the mighty and the perishing of the weapons of war. Their names may live for evermore but their characters are clouded by the preoccupations of succeeding generations.

A short appreciation of the character of Napoleon Bonaparte.

"For our adversary the Devil goeth about like a roaring lion seeking whom he may devour". If for the Devil Bonaparte is substituted it would give a very fair picture of the Napoleonic era. He was the bogeyman of Europe but it must not be forgotten as the song has it that "Boney was a warrior". How much bogeyman and how much warrior this short appreciation will try to decide.

In moments of stress Bonaparte would hum the song "Malbrook se va t'en guerre", and it was Marlborough to whom he turned for inspiration. The military mind does not move quickly and this slowness, combined with the fact that the heads of the European states were also pretty slow movers, makes any soldier who was capable of grasping these two factors appear a military genius.

Marlborough's march to the Danube and Napoleon's march across Europe, which culminated at Austerlitz are obvious evidence. The general who can move has immense superiority over the static one.

Napoleon's mistakes were not for lack of movement. "He has fooled me by God", said Wellington when he realised before Quatre Bras that Bonaparte had gained twenty-four hours on him. This was strategy but where was the equivalent tactical brilliance? Again at Marengo, Desaix's fortunate arrival saved the day whilst Grouchy's peregrinations at Waterloo perhaps lost it.

It would be tedious to cite further examples of tactical lapses. The one great strategic blunder is obvious and the Russian winter cannot entirely take the blame.

Upbringing, political opportunism, a flair for propaganda and a genius for organisation; these combined created the bogeyman image. Self-delusion, in which must be included a lack of appreciation of the British character, brought down the warrior.

A writer of one of the letters reproduced in this book asks Wellington during the occupation of Paris after Waterloo, what he then thought of Bonaparte as a general and whether the result of the late operations had raised or lowered his opinion of Bonaparte's military talents. Wellington said his opinion of Bonaparte remained unchanged; that there was nothing very rare or extraordinary in him as a general; that he always thought him a great glutton, fighting very hard to carry a particular point but showing no resource if his main attack failed; that at Waterloo he had kept driving at the two villages and the ground between them as long as he could get his troops to advance to the attack; that in all this there was very little manoeuvering and nothing of what would formerly be called generalship either in the conception of the plan or in the execution of it. He asked him if he thought Bonaparte very different from or superior to his Marshals. He said no, it appeared to him to be very much the same thing.

Wellington, it must be admitted, was not given to handing out laurels. This appraisal of his adversary rather confirms the truth of this side of his character. Wellington himself admitted later in his life that he had not praised enough. It is certain that there is no vain glory in the criticism which was indeed true of Napoleon's performance at Waterloo.

Bonaparte believed in his star. By 1815 it was very low on the horizon and as we all know, "The fault, dear Brutus, lies not in our stars but in ourselves . . .".

Napoleon

APPENDIX TWO: WELLINGTON

A short appreciation of the character of the Duke of Wellington.

It is the fashion today to debunk or to find some moral flaw in the character of the great or for that matter the not so great. So much has been written about Wellington and so much more about Napoleon that further comment might seem superfluous.

This short appreciation of the Duke's character makes no attempt to carry out the requisite of the first sentence; indeed it would not be necessary. 'Publish and be damned' was his attitude and he never tried to cover up his attachments to women either innocent or not.

Besides his flirtations with the young he had an evident leaning towards affairs with the not so young and by no means innocent, as witness Grassini, the singer; Harriet Wilson, the courtesan; and Lady Caroline Lamb, the notorious.

This side of his character, and others which will be seen later, surely explode the myth of the Iron Duke. History is, of course, written by the opposition and this idea of the hard, inflexible man of iron was certainly a Whig image created during his later somewhat infelicitous political career.

That Wellington was a great man is indisputable, one of the greatest Englishmen that ever lived. Half London is witness to this. He is possibly England's greatest general. Field Marshall Wavell in his famous Lees Knowles lectures on "Generals and Generalship" given in Cambridge in 1939 says:- "This is the first and true function of the leader never to think the battle or the cause lost", and again "But it doesn't matter to a general whether he has his men's affection so long as he has their confidence. He must certainly never court popularity. If he has their appreciation and respect it is sufficient. Efficiency in a general his soldiers have a right to expect, geniality they have a right to suspect. Marlborough was perhaps the only great general to whom geniality was always natural". This was, of course, written before World War II.

It was said of Wavell that his mere presence could raise morale. How much more could that be said of the Duke of Wellington. To the troops he was the long-nosed bugger that beats the French or just simply 'Atty'. To the officers he was the 'Beau' or the 'Peer'. Wellington was too aristocratic, too aloof to desire any mass show of affection such as being cheered; but this is not to say that he did not need personal affection. His wife was a goose whom he had married out of an over developed sense of duty. It is said that of all his female attachments only one was really serious and this came to nothing since the lady was happily married. In view of the fact that all the great beauties of the day set their caps at him this unknown is surprising in one who was so susceptible to women.

Like many commanders since, possibly in imitation, he gathered round him a band of trusted young men who acted as his staff and ADCs. This is no sublimated form of homosexuality (or if so it is no great matter), but a genuine need for companionship which perhaps only the young can give. War at the top can be a lonely business. So many were lost at Waterloo that when the casualty list was brought to him he wept. Dr. Arnold was not yet Headmaster of Rugby and men were not coerced by a rigid system to restrain their feelings.

All his life Wellington was devoted to other people's children, if not particularly to his own. He could be genial among friends, liked parties and entertainments of all kinds but an unopportune phrase or incident or an over bumptious person could be withered with a single look.

It has already been said that the Duke was perhaps England's greatest general. This is, of course, open to dispute as is any bald statement of such a kind. In conclusion, however, I quote with much gratitude from Corelli Barnett's *Napoleon*. "Now at last he (Napoleon) found himself face to face with the English. And no man better exemplified the best qualities of the English ruling class than the Duke of Wellington, with his high-nosed aristocratic confidence and direct simplicity of speech and manners; a man remarkable for high minded good sense, steady nerve and a character as true and tough as the metal of a cannon. In Wellington, Bonaparte had come up against an officer with a simple resolve to do his duty. In Wellington also Bonaparte had come up against by far the most formidable opponent of his career, alike because of the Englishman's professionalism, his force of leadership and his strength of will."

The cannon's casing may be of iron but it must not be forgotten that it is within that the charge is fired. It is then and there that the transformation takes place.

Wellington

APPENDIX THREE:

Lord Whitworth

Lord Whitworth had already had a most distinguished career first in Poland and then in Russia. He is described as being "highly favoured by nature and his address exceeded even his figure. At every period of his life queens, duchesses and countesses have showered on him their regard". It is no wonder, therefore, that he should have been popular at the court of Catherine the Great.

His chief work however was carried out under her successor Paul I. Whitworth was in Russia for twelve years and the many changes in Russian policy towards France taxed his diplomatic skill to its utmost.

Before his appointment to Paris in September 1802 Whitworth had married the widow of the Duke of Dorset, his former patron. As this lady was a great heiress, the new Ambassador to the France of the First Consul was financially fully able to maintain the considerable splendour considered necessary, especially since a long period had elapsed since a British Ambassador had been seen in France.

As has been said the terms of the Peace of Amiens had not been kept by either side, England being especially determined to hold Malta; but during the first two months after Whitworth's arrival there seemed to be a tacit agreement to avoid disagreeable subjects. Napoleon ignored the attacks in the English press, the retention of Malta, and the protracted evacuation of Egypt. Meanwhile England kept silent over the recent French aggressions in Holland, Piedmont, Elba, Parma and Switzerland. The British Government were however obstinate in their refusal to quit Malta until a guarantee had been signed by the various powers ensuring the possession of the Island to the Knights of St. John. This difficulty, which constituted the darkest cloud on the diplomatic horizon, was first raised by Talleyrand on 27 January 1803. Three days later a report was published in the "Moniteur" from Colonel Sabastiani, who had been sent to Egypt by Napoleon on a special mission of enquiry. In this report military information was freely interspersed with remarks disparaging to England, in which country the document was plausibly interpreted as the preface to a second invasion of Egypt by the French. The Addington ministry consequently instructed Whitworth to stiffen his back against any demand for the prompt evacuation of Malta.

On 18 February Napoleon summoned the Ambassador and after the usual stormy outburst of rhetoric, concluded with the memorable appeal, "Let us unite rather than fight and we will together order the destiny of the world".

Any significance that this offer might have had was more than neutralized by the First Consul's observation, "These are mere nothings", when in answer to reproaches about Malta, Whitworth hinted at the increase of French power to Piedmont, Switzerland and elsewhere.

As has been said, this crisis of extreme importance in the career of Napoleon as well as in the history of England came to a head on 13 March 1803.

Contrary to popular belief this was not the final interview between the two men. The Ambassador was received once again on 4 April when the Diplomatic Corps were kept waiting for four hours while Napoleon inspected knapsacks. "When that ceremony was performed he received us, and I had every reason to be satisfied with his manner towards me", so wrote Whitworth to the Foreign Secretary on the same day. War was declared on 18 May 1803.

Napoleon described Whitworth as a "fort bel homme" (memorial de St Helène...). Also at St. Helena in July 1817 he alluded to him as "habile" and "adroit" but always maintained that the accepted version of the encounter was "plein de faussetés".

After Paris Lord Whitworth did not hold another diplomatic post but became Lord Lieutenant of Ireland from 1813 to 1817.

After the Restoration of the Bourbons he visited Paris in April 1819 on what was called "a mission of observation" and in the following October went to Naples in a similar capacity.

He died on 13 May 1825 without issue and all his honours and titles became extinct.

Marquess of Anglesey

APPENDIX FOUR

Obituary of Benjamin Sydenham, Esq. Reproduced from *The Gentleman's Magazine*

March 15. At Bruges, in his 52nd year, after enduring for many years great bodily sufferings, Benjamin Sydenham, Esq., formerly a Commissioner of the Board of Excise.

This gifted and accomplished gentleman was the eldest son of the late Gen., Sydenham, and *entered life* in the engineer corps of the India Company. After serving a few years in India, where his distinguished talents and prepossessing manners introduced him to the notice and intimacy of Lord Wellesley, at that time Governor-General, Mr. Sydenham returned to England with his Lordship, and shortly afterwards obtained an appointment of Commissioner at the Board of Excise. Having from his birth a feeble constitution, though with a fine person, and a temper the most cheerful and elastic, his health was not equal to the mingled pressure of active business and of those seductive and undermining habits which were almost unavoidable for a member of society so much liked and sought after as Mr. Sydenham, in the choicest circles of the convivial world. About the year 1819, his constitution had given way so completely, that he found it impossible to continue any longer the discharge of his official duties, and retired to the continent. Mr Sydenham was a gentleman of polished manners and of exquisite taste in the arts. His animated and interesting conversation was enlivened by anecdote, and improved by various knowledge; to these social qualifications he united uncommon buoyancy of spirit under every change of scene and circumstance, great warmth and steadiness in his attachments, and a kindly recollection even of those whom he might, without the reproach of injustice or ingratitude, have forgotten.

Prussian Cavalry

APPENDIX FIVE

Memoir of Thomas Sydenham, Esq. Reproduced from *The Gentleman's Magazine*

Aug. 28. Died, at Geneva, after long and painful bodily sufferings, borne with exemplary fortitude, in his 37th year, Thomas Sydenham, Esq., second son of the late General Sydenham, Military Auditor General, and afterwards Commandant of artillery at Madras. He was educated at Harrow, and went to India in 1794, where he speedily made himself master of the Arabic and Persian languages, keys respectively to the learning and politeness of the East. From the confidential and responsible, though subordinate office of Captain of Guides in the Mysore war, he was selected by Lord Wellesley, to whom he was personally unknown, but purely on the score of his high reptutation, to be Secretary to the Residency of Hyderabad - a critical post in the Government of India, while the territory of Tippoo was a recent conquest. This he was compelled to resign in 1802, on account of ill health; and came to England, where he gave a singular proof of industry, good taste, and ambition to improve himself, by hastening to Oxford at the age of 22, where, under the protection of Dr. Jackson, the venerable Dean of Christ Church, he diligently and successfully prosecuted his studies. On his return to India in 1804, Mr. Sydenham was nominated by Marquis Wellesley to take charge of the British Residency at Persia; and afterwards, on that Nobleman's warm recommendation, he was appointed our Minister at Hyderabad. This situation he resigned in 1810, on experiencing what he considered an act of injustice on the part of the Supreme Government of India during the unhappy mutiny. His general conduct was, however, highly approved, both by Lord Minto and the Court of Directors. On Mr. Sydenham's second return to England he was sent by Marquis Wellesley on a confidential mission to the Duke of Wellington; thence appointed Chargé d'Affaires at Lisbon; and shortly afterwards joined the Commissioners for mediating between Old Spain and her Colonies; in which capacity he went round with Sir George Cockburn to Cadiz. Mr. Sydenham, Esq., joined the Duke of Wellington, and served as a volunteer through nearly the whole of the arduous campaign of 1812. Towards the close of the year last mentioned he was offered by Lord Bathurst the mission to Morocco, which he declined; he repaired in 1813 to the headquarters of the Russian army, and served the campaign of 1814 with his friend Count Michel Woronzow, who now commanded the Russian corps of occupation within the French territory. His skill and gallantry were here conspicuous, and so greatly distinguished him at the battle of Craon amongst others, as to procure him from the hands of the Emperor Alexander the cross of the Imperial

Order of St. George; and from Bernadotte, to whom his steady patron, Lord Wellesley, had strongly recommended him, the Swedish insignia of the Sword. The last public character which this amiable man obtained was that of British Envoy Extraordinary and Minister Plenipotentiary to Lisbon; to which he was promoted in 1814. At Lisbon he was not long enabled to execute those duties for which, by his knowledge of Portugal, he was so eminently fitted: for here the fatal illness seized him, which, after two years of indescribable suffering, has borne him to a foreign grave. Those who were not intimately acquainted with Mr. Sydenham would be surprised, were we to enumerate the solidity and variety of those attainments, by which, as a scholar and a man of business, he had prepared his mind both for action and happiness. Besides his perfect knowledge of Oriental languages, he was as familiar with French and Spanish as with his native tongue. He was in habits of confidence and intimacy with the Duke of Wellington, Sir Henry Wellesley, Sir Charles Stuart, the late Duke of Portland, Count Woronzow, and many other eminent characters in various parts of Europe. But his most fortunate acquisition was the steady friendship and patronage of Lord Wellesley, who first introduced him into public life. Nor was this connexion less honourable as it was useful to Mr. Sydenham, who was a total stranger to the noble Marquis; but like several other men of worth, whose conduct has done credit to the discrimination of that Nobleman, he was brought forward by him for his character alone, and because he had no interest to his patron but his personal merit. The favourable sentiments thus excited by his Lordship's official knowledge of Mr. Sydenham's qualifications gradually ripened to feelings of the warmest attachment and regard, which were manifested on numerous occasions, but never in a manner as kind or grateful as during his last fatal illness. The patience and cheerfulness of temper exhibited by the subject of the present memoir may be judged of by the fact, that, when perishing under the last attack of anasarca, and a prey to almost hourly pangs of suffocation, he enjoyed the charms of musick and society to within a few hours of his dissolution. The night before he expired, he had a concert in his room, and on his friends taking leave of him, he fell into a tranquil slumber from which he never awoke. Mr Thomas Sydenham has left behind him an elder brother, who is a Commissioner of Excise; one younger, in India (Capt. Sydenham) political agent at Aurunga; and a sister, Mrs Ross, wife of Col. Ross, of the 75th regiment, now in the Ionian Isles.

Lord Hill